Living Inside your Passion

by

Robert P. Theiss

Eugene, Oregon USA

Ancient Wings®

The Teachings of Michael

Products and Services

Living Inside your Passion
Straddling your Freedom
Writing Journals - Gratitude Series
Greeting Cards - Earth and Goddess Series

The Teachings of Michael

Friends of Spirit Program
Home Study Courses
Sessions with Spirit
Channel Library

Please Visit:
ancientwings.com and sanctuarydesigns.blogspot.com

Living Inside your Passion
By Robert P. Theiss

Copyright © 2009 by Robert P.Theiss
ISBN 978-0-578-00664-2
Published by Ancient Wings
P.O. Box 1148
North Plains, Oregon 97133

Design: Ancient Wings
Editorial supervision: Gena Duel
Cover images: Koka Filipovic
Interior chapter heading image: Agb
Backcover photo: Shirley Collins

About the Author

Robert openly shares a conscious relationship he has developed with Spirit, including the presence of Archangel Michael, Yeshua and Father Spirit. He is an internationally recognized artist, author and healer who teaches with compassion, humor and joy. His messages are always uplifting, self-empowering and based in Love. He has served and shared the Teachings of Michael since 1998 and is the founder and director of Ancient Wings® and the Choosing Balance™Program.

Ancient Wings
P.O. Box 1148
North Plains, Oregon 97133
Email: info@ancientwings.com
www.ancientwings.com

Cover Art: Koka Filipovic
www.sanctuarydesigns.blogspot.com

Acknowledgements

This book is dedicated to all the new teachers and
healers who embrace life with joy and passion.
Your presence on this planet is a blessing to all of life.
Thank you!

Contents

Chapter One

Living on Earth

    My dreams of late have been about dancing. They often take place in a beautiful park surrounded by old growth trees, flowers in full bloom and hundreds of birds singing. It's just another ideal day to be alive on Earth.

    In this dream I see myself acting like an android - very predictable, mechanical, and looking a little out of place in this setting. I look at my surroundings and begin to label and identify everything as being separate from myself. This seems to make me feel more comfortable with this environment. I've been programmed to perceive physical reality as being the only reality. I've been taught to view life as a series of opposing forces of good and evil, light and dark. I learned to put my mind to the grindstone, work hard, and for that I am rewarded with a vacation once a year for being a good person. Life inside this android self feels safe. I know what is real, what is expected of me and how to accomplish what needs to be done. In general, I am also kind and respectful of others, but I feel uncomfortable if I am asked to participate in anything I haven't learned. My android self has begun to feel very stressed out lately with the responsibility of keeping this known world intact. Compounding this dilemma is a growing, annoying feeling that I am also bored. In the silence of my mind, my android self calls for help.

In the distance, I notice someone walking towards me. It's a beautiful woman walking barefoot who begins to freely dance the closer she gets. Her movements are graceful, passionate, and flowing. She begins to twirl, leans back, and laughs as her hair flows within the currents of a gentle breeze. Suddenly she leaps into the air. It appears for a moment that she is suspended in time while she gently turns her gaze at me. My android self is spell bound by her presence and very confused. As she approaches me the confusion turns into fear. Although her features are very unique, her face is identical to my own.

She begins to dance in circles around my body, gently touching and caressing my face. Suddenly she stops, looks directly into my android eyes, and whispers into my ear - I love you! Dance with me! A rush of new feelings overwhelm my android self as she takes my hand and begins to guide me in a series of slow, deliberate movements. I keep tripping over my own feet and begin to feel embarrassed. She holds my head up while staring deeply into my eyes and proclaims again - I love you! How could this be? How could I be looking at myself and yet have nothing in common with this dancer? My android self stops moving, looks back at her and asks - "who are you?" Her eyes begin to blaze with such a passion unlike anything my android self has ever seen. At first it frightens my android self, then suddenly her eyes become as still as a lake, reflecting a deep and profound compassion for the state of my android self. She turns to me and proclaims, "I am called consciousness. I reside within all of creation, including you! You called me. I offer myself to be a part of your life."

I suddenly wake up and begin to laugh. Okay, I get it, I say to anyone who might be listening. I believe many of us share this dream and also struggle with allowing our own consciousness to be a part of our conditioned reality. These are very exciting times to be living on Earth. The changes that are taking place can be very unsettling, but within each of us resides the solution to all of our problems.

The heart of this book represents a multifaceted relationship I share with a spiritual family called the Family of Michael. It has become my passion and joy to share this relationship in our workshops and sessions. At the heart of this family resides the presence of archangel Michael. He offers his hand in friendship and his heart in communion to any human being to help heal the separation between Earth, our soul families, and source energy.

I dedicate this book to you, dear reader. You are the ones who are willing to embrace and integrate consciousness into your life. You are the ones who will inspire others to reconnect with their own soul nature. It takes tremendous compassion, integrity, and a very good sense of humor to experience life outside our conditioned story.

I believe that all of us share a common desire to experience a direct relationship with the source of life. It is a profound experience that enables us to serve life with joy and passion. Now is the time to live inside those passions, create the life your heart truly desires and discover the beauty of your own soul. Let the conscious dance begin.

Robert Theiss

Chapter Two

*Living Inside
your
Passion*

As we blend our presence with our partner, I Michael invite each of you to embrace this moment as another opportunity to experience how it feels when you allow life to serve you. Life loves to serve itself! If you are willing to claim this as being your truth, your life will be showered by a newfound joy and passion. All that your heart desires is not a fairytale. It is a dynamic, new relationship with life that is initiated by choice.

Radiating out from the hearts and minds of the human family is a consistent chorus - why are we here? Why have we forgotten who we are? If it is true that we volunteered to be here, why would we choose such a challenging experience?

Let's take a journey back in time to reflect upon these important questions. We remind you that the majority of your existence has been spent in the stars as a nonphysical being. What would inspire you to leave a reality that for the most part keeps you connected to your angelic roots?

Your soul remembers a time long ago when you resided in a grand and beautiful place that we call the kingdom. Here you embodied unity consciousness. In the kingdom you never experienced yourself as being separate from life. You had no idea what fear was. It was completely unknown to you. Every moment was another opportunity to bask in the unconditional love radiating from the father and mother aspects of creation. You were surprised and deeply honored when they turned to their children and offered the same abilities they embodied with the freedom to use them in any way you desired. They invited you to become independent creators that embodied an unconditional love for life.

You see, the Father/Mother aspects discovered their love for life could not be contained, even within this blissful, serene environment called the kingdom. Their understanding of love and their joy for sharing their love inspired them to set their creations free, without conditions. They asked each of you souls if you would be willing to become the new explorers of life outside the realms of the kingdom. They offered to share all of their creative abilities with each of you, an aspect of themselves that we call your divine nature. You would become independent, sovereign creators yet interconnected to the source of life. You were offered complete freedom to use these unlimited, creative abilities in any way you desired - serving a love for life that could not be contained!

Now, there are many stories about the origins of life. Our words cannot do justice to the multidimensional experience you encountered when you left the kingdom. Since that time, each of you remember the kingdom with a deep yearning to return "home," to the blissful, ecstatic environment that supported you. You have spent eons of time struggling to make peace with this new freedom, fine tuning, like an artist, your creative abilities. Each of you are living examples of source energy with the ability to create life. The Father/Mother aspects of creation do not spend one moment feeling concerned about your choices. There was no fine print in their offer, you have complete freedom to create life as you choose it for yourself.

You are some of the first cosmic artists. True creators! Like all artists, it takes time to develop your skills and understand your preferences. Many of your early creations you judged to be imperfect but unlike a human artist, you couldn't simply destroy your work and start over. Your creations or life forms continued to live their life just as they are. For the first time, you experienced feeling responsible for your own creations. You judged your creations to lack the self awareness that would grant them the kind of freedom you enjoyed.

Living Inside your Creations

A co-creator that begins to distrust their creative abilities is not a pretty site. Some of you began to feel that the freedom you now embodied was more of a burden than a gift. Your reaction to your new independent nature and your self judgment about your creative abilities initiated some new feelings. You experienced guilt, resentment and self doubt for the first time. Many of you, while living in the stars were determined to resolve this growing inner conflict. Together, you began to descend your consciousness into realities that gave you a more tangible reflection of your own inner environment. The most tangible reflection is here on Earth. This planet provides the opportunity for your soul to experience itself within its own creations. It takes a truly magnificent and courageous artist to want to acknowledge and validate how their inner reality is shaping their external experience.

Now, if this experiment were easy all of creation would have signed up. The history of the human species gives graphic evidence that Earth is a place truly for masters. Now we know the story of humanity is often turned upside down suggesting it is more like a penal colony for misfits. We often share how much we enjoy kissing your feet. We do so to acknowledge the creator within you. When we proclaim that your life on Earth serves all of life, we want you to feel our love for the divine artists who are learning to set their creations free. You learn this as a human being in all of the roles you play in your personal relationships. The mother or father that sets their children free by trusting that life will support them. The employer that offers complete freedom to its employees to explore their creative abilities, trusting that it will add to the well being of the company. The citizen that sets its government free by taking responsibility for their own life. The spiritual teacher that sets its students free by trusting in the divine nature within all souls. You, beloved human being, are here on Earth at this time to reclaim your divine nature. You are learning to trust in your inherent, creative abilities and impulses while discovering a new joy for life when you stop feeling responsible for your creations! A responsible creator sets their creations free!

In your human affairs, you play out these galactic issues in all of your relationships. When you feel responsible for the lives of others, you are willing to process for them what you believe they are unable to do for themselves. You energetically process the unresolved issues of your children to free them of their pain. You do the same with your partners, husbands and wives, friends and co-workers. You have become such experts at processing energies that you believe you can process the unresolved issues for entire communities, countries, and this planet. This very relationship has delayed many of the natural changes Gaia needs to experience in order to move and change her own energetic relationship with life.

Now, we understand why some of you would choose to process these generational issues. You share this planet with all of humanity and prefer an environment that is not quaking and shaking. It is only when your body begins to break down that you also begin to question the wisdom behind your intentions. Compounded by the lack of recognition for this type of sacrificial work you perform for others, you begin to honor your purpose for being on Earth

- to resolve your relationship with your creative abilities in whatever form they take.

I Love my Life

How do the Father/Mother aspects of creation, the source of life or God/Goddess/All That Is feel about them self? We would say it begins with a simple truth. At the core of their existence, all aspects of your origins joyfully proclaim, moment to moment - I Love my Life! I am That I am and I love my life! We are That we Are and We love Life! God Is and God loves all of life! It is a profound truth and we invite each of you as human beings to openly proclaim this truth by FEELING the energy behind these simple words. I LOVE MY LIFE! Practice saying this until it begins to feel real. Begin to consciously breathe the energy of loving your life with every breath you take.

Again, you choose to be here to live within your creations, your creative abilities. You are not being punished, although from the outside it would appear you are punishing yourself. Many get lost in this experience by waiting for their life to begin to feel better before they are willing to proclaim their love for life. We invite you to begin practicing saying this simple truth to yourself no matter what you are experiencing in your life. Having a bad hair day? I LOVE MY LIFE! Wishing a coworker would leave the planet? I LOVE MY LIFE! Your bank account has no money in it - I LOVE MY LIFE!

Lets apply this truth to your life in a practical manner. Devote 30 minutes to choosing to become a conscious observer of how the energy from this statement about yourself can change your life. Begin by repeating "I love my life" and continue repeating this until you feel or sense a new joy. Start to breathe that joy in with each breath and claim this experience to be valid. Value it like you value your purse or wallet. Now notice during the next 30 minutes how your mind and the voices from your past will attempt to distract your attention. You might notice yourself slowly entering a trance like state that has you forgetting how good it feels when you do love your life. You might hear thoughts that will encourage you to focus your attention on unfulfilled desires, deadlines and goals. Just observe this internal swirl of activity and notice that every time you claim love for your life the energy shifts. It brings you back into this moment, freed of your past conditions and open to new adventures. After 30 minutes there is no need to stop, please continue.

Humanity uses the term enlightenment to describe a profound and conscious connection with source energy. Loving yourself in this manner is a potent exercise in reestablishing that connection for yourself. Enlightenment is your willingness to love your life in this moment, just as you are. This acceptance awakens your relationship with your divine nature and over time you will become a sovereign, independent aspect of source; God/Goddess/All That Is!

Life on Earth is a backdrop for you to resolve your galactic dilemma. Owning the joy from declaring that you love your life, no matter where you are in your life, will serve to break the dualistic patterns of thought that keep you from claiming this freedom. The freedom to experience life in way your heart desires. The freedom to experience unity consciousness, not as you knew this to be in the kingdom as fear did not exist in that reality. Unity consciousness living outside the kingdom is all about making peace with complete opposites. How does a conditioned human being dance with the unlimited nature of the soul? It would appear from the outside that such a dance is impossible. Each and every time your human nature allows your divinity to co-exist in its life, you model unity consciousness at work outside the kingdom. You offer a solution to a polarized, galactic dilemma that separates love from fear, light from dark, and right from wrong. All because you allowed the divine presence of life to come to you!

I Love to Share my Creations

Declaring that you love your life creates a foundation that now supports expressing that love. Your divine nature loves itself and all of its creations unconditionally. It embraces an understanding that knows love cannot be contained. This is very important - love cannot be contained! It could not be contained within the environment of the kingdom or anywhere else in all of existence. As a creator, you honor love each and every time you share your creations. As a human being, this simple truth will serve to set your abundance issues free.

Now, we already anticipate your next question – how do we do this? Let's imagine that many of you have a product or service that you feel inspired to share with the world. Being a lover of life, you begin to feel a new relationship with your product or service. You start to practice conscious breathing, You begin to feel the presence of joy fill your life and overflow into your product or service. With every inhale you are literally breathing life into your body and with each exhale you are sharing the same life force with your own creations. Your products or service are now infused with the same life that supports your body and, they begin to develop a life of their own.

Your creation is now blessed by your willingness to trust in your creative abilities, but your product or service cannot be contained. Like the Mother/Father aspects of creation, to honor the nature of love you set them free by sharing them with your world. The product or service is indeed your creation, but your service is to love. They are simply the vehicle for loved to be shared. Take a moment to "feel" the value in this statement.

The joy you experience from loving your life opens your imagination to endless possibilities of how to serve or share your new creation. Now, the mind will intervene and suggest that all this joy will lead you down the road to la la land. Yes - well, welcome home! You have a very important choice to make when it's time to share your creations. Will your conditioned human nature, your old story, try to control how you share, distribute and market your creations? If so, be prepared to work very hard and receive very little. You can also choose to act on any of the endless possibilities, acknowledge the resistance you feel from the voices from your past, and continue to act while you proclaim - I LOVE MY LIFE!

Your comfort zones will be challenged when you make a choice to serve the nature of love. Serving love will invite all of life to also serve you and will require of you to say - YES! Even when your knees are weak and your head is spinning with fear practice proclaiming -I love my life! You will find yourself saying yes to a variety of opportunities that expose your creations. If it's about YOU, seeking

recognition and approval from outside yourself, your creations will become polarized - held in place by your own
fears and limitations. We want you to understand this
point. When you truly open yourself to feeling an authentic
love for your life, life "will" respond. You will be offered
opportunities that will challenge how your conditioned
human nature will try to contain your creative abilities and
expressions.

I Love Receiving

A spiritual foundation that begins with self love
naturally extends into sharing your love for life and is
complimented by a willingness to receive love. Your divine
nature does not avoid being recognized, it joyfully embraces all reflections of its creative nature. Simply put, it is
not shy.

Many of you that have been on your own spiritual
journey for some time have developed an awareness of the
nature of your ego self and know how it feels when your
soul nature is at play. We honor your sense of integrity
when it comes to not wanting to misrepresent the authentic nature of your soul. You fear that your own ego will use
your creations to receive from others what it doesn't have
within itself - love. Being on the receiving end of life is a
natural part of your creation process. Watch how you use

shyness to filter this type of recognition, which tends to do exactly what you fear. It brings your personality/ego to the forefront.

You can practice being in receivership in a number of ways. We mentioned in our book (Riding a Stallion) how receiving some form of body work or massage on a regular basis can help you grow comfortable with allowing life to support you. This too is self love. It will awaken your connection to your divine nature and release your doubts surrounding your creative abilities. The next time someone wants to compliment your work, notice how your energy pulls back, recoils to protect what? Perhaps you are feeling your own judgment about the imperfection of your own creations to avoid the potential rejection. Those of you that have walked away from trying to become prefect are very wise indeed!

The year of 2008 was all about creating new potentials. Allowing yourself to imagine new opportunities by living outside your story. Self love is a story waiting to be lived. 2009 will invite each of you to act on these new potentials now as a lover of life. A time will come when it is your turn to leave this planet. The only thing you take with you are your experiences. If you attempt to cling to your creations or your relationships you will find that transition a little awkward. Life invites you to create whatever your heart desires and to set it free. Many of you are just beginning to experience this newfound freedom and recognize this lifetime as being your last. All of you have enticed millions of souls to now visit Earth for the first time. You are demonstrating how polarized opposites can coexist. Your conditioned human nature is beginning to dance with your unconditional divine nature. Your conditioned galactic nature is beginning to dance with your divine nature. Your life on Earth is a work of art for all to witness, a living example of how to resolve the inner conflicts of a conscious co-creator. We, the Family of Michael, bow before the new divine artists who will leave this Earth, look out at the stars and like a blank canvas begin to create life freed from your self judgements.

Many souls will now feel inspired to experience their life on Earth for the first time because you were willing to live outside your story. The story of creation is indeed profound, but it is just a story. In a way, it seems to be repeating itself. From your experience here on Earth, you have developed a profound wisdom. Each of you carry the gift of life and within this universe you have come to embrace, share and receive the reflections of your gift to life. Life now serves you because you were willing to serve love by loving you!

Chapter Three

Embracing Your Human Aspects

It is an honor for us to once again blend our presence with our many friends here on Earth. There is a small but very determined group of human beings who want more than anything else to experience the profound nature of their soul. This group is not only creating new potentials for themselves but for future generations on Earth. I, Michael and the presence of Sananda celebrate your desire to experience the freedom of joy. We invite you to trust in your own abilities to resolve the limitations you inherited. The path of least resistance invites your soul to sit in the front seat and assume responsibility for your life. Change can happen very quickly when you stop asking your conditioned aspects to shoulder your burdens. As you free yourself from the restraints of your past, you can safely begin to explore your multifaceted, multidimensional nature.

We have been speaking about your human nature, your personality, for some time. This conditioned identity has a long standing invitation to live alongside your unconditional nature. Some have suggested that you must remove, purge or evict this personality from your life in order to experience the true essence of your soul. The soul however has the ability to embrace all of life as being interconnected. At the very core of your soul resides a most precious aspect of creation called your divinity. This part of you "knows" itself to be God/Goddess/All That Is. It knows this for it "IS" this. Many of you have experienced the energetic presence of your divinity and yearn to deepen that relationship. You feel frustrated at times by the process that would allow you to integrate that connection into your day-to-day reality. We remind you that humanity is at the very beginning stage of this grand shift in consciousness. We perceive your quantum leap as it integrates into the collective consciousness of humanity occurring during the next 200 years. Shifting a pattern of energy that has existed on Earth for eons in a matter of two centuries appears to us as being quite the leap. Change can indeed happen very quickly for the individual who chooses to be at the forefront of this shift. Integrating this dramatic change does take time, compassion and patience.

Our teaching has always been about embracing your soul nature. For the last 10 years we have invited you to acknowledge the patterns of behavior that interfere with your passions. Many of you believed you found a shortcut by denying the existence of your conditioned nature and the role it plays in your life. There is a fast lane in this ascension process. It embraces how you feel and supports conscious choices to stop reacting, start feeling and begin living a life that includes the presence of your soul. At face value, it would appear that these two opposites, your conditioned and unconditional aspects, are not compatible. There is a lot of energy residing in your conditioned aspects that makes you feel very uncomfortable. If you would allow yourself to "feel" that these conditioned aspects are also your soul mates, change can happen very quickly. We have labeled the collective consciousness of these aspects as being your personality. We would like to share how we believe they can coexist, like roommates living in your body that feels very much like a five bedroom house. A room for your child, adolescent, adult, body and soul.

The Child

Your early childhood represented a time when your connection to your soul and your nonphysical family was still intact. Your perception of reality, as a child, would frighten many of you as an adult. These were your preconditioned years. The magical child was alive and well. When you reached the age of 4-6 years old, the magical child was initiated into becoming the conditioned child. You entered a period of socialization from your educational and, for some, religious institutions. It was during this period that you inherited many of your personal beliefs about life. It was also during this period that your soul's connection became very fragile. Your soul had one foot in your body and one foot in our reality. The pain from experiencing love withheld made it very difficult for the soul to stay embodied. We honor the child that was forced to become less then itself in order to survive the environment placed before it. We honor the child that was forced to adapt to the expectations of those around you. In a room in your house that you call your body, behind closed doors lives this child.

The Adolescent

Your identity took another leap at around 13-16 years old. Your adolescence offered a pivotal and potent time for personal growth and empowerment. This was truly a time to celebrate a new found freedom that allowed the dynamic presence of your soul to once again be a part of your identity by developing a truly sovereign relationship with life. Many of you gave yourself permission to express your suppressed feelings and to begin to act on your creative impulses. In a healthy culture, you would be honored with a rite of passage, shifting your relationship with those that played the role as your parent and teacher. A time that would ask your culture to step forward and model a truly sovereign and fulfilled human being. We recognize and honor the feelings of this adolescent aspect of your human identity that was never given its rite of passage. It continues to project its anger and resentment into your personal and intimate relationships. It feels it was never given permission to allow the soul to be in its life. It now demands that your husbands, wives, employers and friends become its surrogate parent. In a room in your house that you call your body, behind closed doors lives this adolescent.

The Adult

Your adolescent aspect became tired of the battle for its freedom. Over time it resigned itself to continue playing the game of becoming what others expected you to become. Your society offers countless labels for the many roles you can play. Your self worth became reinforced by how accomplished you became in playing those roles. The adult began to identify with itself as being the mother, father, parent, employee or employer. The roles became your mask that allowed you to suppress the agendas for your child and adolescent aspects. The role became so familiar that most of you started to identify yourself as becoming the mask you were wearing.

A time comes in your life when the soul once again makes its presence known. Sometimes you experience a severe change in your life that gives you the opportunity to reexamine your choices. You begin to feel that the mask you are wearing is so thin. You begin to pursue a more authentic relationship with life. You yearn for the magical child and wonder how it would feel to have that presence in your life. The adult becomes conscious of how conditioned its responses to life have become. It begins to practice spiritual teachings that serve to reconnect its life with your soul. An unexpected result takes place. Suddenly the doors of your child and adolescent identities fly open. The child recognizes the soul as being the magic it lost. The adolescent recognizes the soul as being the model of a sovereign identity it never became. Your adult self becomes conscious of how the child just wants to play. The adolescent self wants its rite of passage. It wants to be acknowledged for being emotionally 13-16 years old. It doesn't have the capacity to assume responsibility for your life. The unresolved issues of your child and adolescent aspects become entrenched agendas that seek fulfillment in all of your relationships. The adult wisely seeks healing practices that encourage reuniting these aspects within you, giving them a voice to express their anger. Inside your house, behind closed doors lives this adult trying so hard to discover itself in the role it has been playing.

The Body

Your body, this house where all of your human aspects reside, reflects the consciousness of these roommates with its own community of cells. As these aspects change, so must the cells. What you call ascension, we call allowing your soul to become a roommate. It changes everything including the nature of your cells. They now must reflect the presence of your soul, which isn't good news to the cells that have fed on the habitual nature of your aspects. Your body consciousness is a living reflection of your household. Spiritual growth allows the soul to become the head of this household without any control issues.

The Soul

We use the term soul to describe the I AM presence that exists at the very core of its nature. The I AM presence knows without any doubt that it too is God/Goddess/ALL THAT IS. The soul embodies the mind, your male nature and your female nature - consciousness. Your soul nature is multifaceted, multidimensional and it radiates from its core an immense love for life.

As a human being, what you term to be your higher self is but an aspect of your soul nature. Your higher self or grander self allowed itself to divide into 12 aspects of itself to be compatible with your human biology; such is your magnificence. If your higher self represents the nature of your soul within this universe, then it too is but an aspect of a grander self that exists within this known galaxy. Aspects of your soul allow your soul nature to travel within a variety of realities. Some of your grander selves exist within realities to simply "be." Creation, however, continues to expand into greater discoveries. Is it enough to simply "be" or do our creations also define our consciousness? Can you not also feel this desire to place your own consciousness within your creations? All is one beloved, no matter how you choose to define it.

Our teaching asks of you to invite these human aspects, including the voice of your body to come out of their rooms and sit together in your living room, the heart of your body. You cannot evict the child, adolescent or adult from your house simply because you don't like their behavior. We find it amusing that many have attempted to relieve themselves of this responsibility by relying on their mental bodies. The mind offers a safe haven to maintain a detached relationship with these aspects or your roommates - detached from having to engage with your own experience.

Exercise

We would like to share a simple exercise that invites each aspect to speak its truth. Begin by making a list of 10 questions that relate to your own life. Next to each question write the name of each of your human aspects. Let yourself go deeply into feeling the child, adult, etc. and write how they each feel about each question. Allow your aspects to speak its truth. Don't judge the feelings. You might be surprised to see who has been controlling your life behind these closed doors. How do we resolve this situation? How do these conditioned aspects learn to coexist and trust the unlimited presence of your soul? We have suggested that you don't take your soul's nature at face value. Put it to the test. Dump all the issues that have been expressed by each one of these aspects at the feet of your soul. Put the unlimited, unconditional nature of your soul to work and witness how this house divided becomes whole again. In a blink of an eye? Of course not. That would deny your ability to integrate this new relationship. It will ask of your child, adolescent and adult to surrender its agendas. Dumping your issues at the feet of your soul doesn't mean your soul will now fulfill all the unfulfilled agendas. Each of these aspects will, over time, learn to trust in the soul the more you acknowledge how they are feeling. The more you rely on the thoughts of your soul and how it feels. When was the last time you truly experienced joy, bliss and ecstasy? Now, how does your soul feel about your life? Are you beginning to experience an enormous pressure to allow change in your life by acting on new desires? Are you beginning to feel an unexpected excitement for living your life with passion? Are you beginning to spend unproductive moments allowing yourself to daydream and imagine new possibilities for your future? Dreaming of a fulfilled life? The thoughts from your soul must also be acknowledged and for them to become real, they must be ACTED ON! The presence of your soul can

take your human nature's breath away. Its capacity to resolve polarized issues is truly amazing. Its ability to
imagine potentials into manifestation is astounding.
Change happens very quickly when you stop relying on the
agendas of your child, adolescent, and adult. We would say
it happens so quickly that your human aspects will label it
as being magic.   The vast majority of humanity lives their entire life on Earth having
never tasted the presence of their soul as an adult. The vast
majority of spiritual seekers want more from life but never
allow the thoughts and feelings from their soul to become
their life. All of your religions were inspired by people just
like you that allowed their soul to become the head of their
household. That relationship appears so radically different
from a house divided that you have called these souls as-
cended masters. We have to laugh, for all of us are still
here, inviting you to consciously participate in a relationship that is very symbolic for how you relate to the many
aspects of your own soul. They are interconnected. Every
time you invite your human aspects to come sit together,
your invitation becomes interdimensional. We have been
speaking of this grand reunion for some time and for many
of you that is happening as we speak.

In this new relationship, the
child within you learns to trust in the nurturing qualities of

your soul and stops projecting that need into your intimate relationships. Over time, the child grows into the teenager that you honor with your own ritual. The adolescent learns to trust in the parenting abilities of your soul and stops projecting its unfulfilled desires into your life, expecting others to play the role of its parent. It discovers that your soul is glad to play the role but not as a victim. It offers a refreshing, direct and honest approach to this new relationship. Over time, it grows into an adult and begins to participate in a life that isn't so rigid. The adult begins to see the folly in all of the roles it has played and over time grows into becoming the soul's lover. The roommates in your house become best friends because you acknowledged their presence, accepted their consciousness and allowed the presence of your soul to become the head of your household.   You become the living model for unity consciousness, demonstrating that complete opposites can coexist. The human angel becomes just that, the conditioned and unconditional living side by side. It is time dear human to take ownership of your thoughts. Not by denying the rightful place of your human aspects or allowing them to control your life. The thoughts of your soul don't demand your attention, they embrace a new and profound passion for living!

Demonstrate to yourself the power of love and its

all encompassing nature. You are so close to tasting the very fruits you desire. Dear human aspects, now would be a very good time to release your attachment to your agendas. Dump all of your issues at the feet of the soul. Each and every time you embrace your human aspects with the presence of your soul, you also invite fragments of your soul to return to their core. An intergalactic family reunion that now meets on a regular basis in your five bedroom house to celebrate a new life. You are loved more than you know!

Chapter Four

A World in Crisis

It comes as no surprise to any of you that your world is in dire need of new leaders, ones who are guided by the heart. Most of your so-called leaders, whether they are elected or self imposed have their own self interests in mind. Many of you have been waiting for a long time, perhaps lifetimes, to witness the changes in your world that your heart desires. Our service, in this lifetime is to remind you that the waiting is over. The changes you desire begin within because within you resides another self imposed leader or dictator. It is guided by fear and attempts to manipulate, undermine and control the direct guidance from your own heart.

The leadership on your planet is changing because so many of you recognized that your heart doesn't require leadership. It follows no one, it serves life knowing itself to "be" the source of life. There are millions living on Earth at this time that fully embrace this concept. There are far less who are living it. Our question to each of you is very simple. Whom do you serve? Do you believe your human family needs more guidance on how to store foods? Indeed! Then what is your joy? Are you willing to give your internal state of being the same value you give to your retirement benefits, bank and savings accounts? Only you have access to your internal account. You can also choose not to value your self and allow others to withdraw energies without your permission. We call this a horizontal relationship with humanity. Only you can deposit energies into this account. Joy is a truly priceless deposit, backed by the unlimited resources of source energy.

We will say it again and again, now is the time to reclaim the throne of your own being. The mind naturally goes into fear when consciousness is not a part of your life. It will always want to rule your external affairs if your internal account isn't valued. Are there major Earth changes in your near future? Yes. The body of Gaia welcomes the presence of your soul. Much like your own human body, it will also need to change some energies to accommodate the immense presence or vibration of your soul nature. Will these Earth changes be devastating? Will your social systems collapse? Step back for a moment and take a deep breath. Beloved, you incarnated upon this planet because it appeared humanity would destroy itself. You volunteered to offer tangible evidence of how a soul enjoys life. The good news, at least from our perspective, is that you are still here. Without your presence, indeed, the future looked very bleak. What you are facing is a complete overhaul of a system that was destined to destroy itself. Such is the folly of a mind that believes itself to be the creator.

There is a real crisis upon your planet and there are also real solutions. These solutions come from those who were willing to look beyond what's already known. The mind will learn to accept a new relationship that puts consciousness in the drivers seat. How does consciousness enter your life? Breathe in this moment! Slowly begin to feel the joy building in your body. Empower yourself with choices that serve this joy. Begin to serve life and your human family. You enrich your life and empower your choices when you also share your gifts. Beloved, you may call yourself a starseed, but you are also interconnected to your human family while sharing the same physical environment. Yes, peace begins within you, but it does not end there! This is your time to "act" on behalf of a new truth that doesn't ask of you to oppose anyone. All life on Earth becomes enriched each and every time you share your gifts. You, beloved, carry the solution humanity is waiting for.

You ask of coming events, indeed! We forewarn all of humanity-love will have its way with this planet! Is that a problem? You, the new leaders must begin to treasure this feeling of joy as being the most precious resource you could ever receive. The mind of humanity will be shouting from rooftops that the world is ending. Indeed, the mind is losing control. The mind within those who have already claimed their heart to be their truth is suggesting - "let's skip the embarrassing part, teach me how to receive my counterpart - consciousness." In human terms we have described this reunion as being two lovers, your male (mind) and female (consciousness) aspects. The world doesn't need yet another voice for fear. Retirement benefits? Mortgage payments? We promise you, if all of that disappeared, life will continue. Your personal safety and security do not reside within a system that is changing. It resides in your willingness to value "being" or feeling in the moment.

Anchoring your Soul

During these times of great change, the solutions that your soul embodies require an anchor point to fully integrate its presence. We suggest you begin your day anchoring (grounding) your body to the center of the Earth. Make a commitment to life by devoting yourself to claiming how YOU want to feel. Yesterday will keep calling to remind you of unfulfilled obligations, worries, and concerns. Freedom comes to each of you when you stop picking up the phone. Your news will continue to highlight major shifts in your institutions that were created by a mind that experienced itself as being separate from love. Anchored to this beautiful planet, your body acts as a personal portal for source energy. Life will continue to serve your internal state. It will support, without question, whatever story you choose to experience.

Serving the Transition

Your planet is just beginning to experience what many of you have known intuitively for some time. We have shared how this polarized relationship with life has created a dualistic reality and from our perspective, has no future. It is contracting upon itself. It is living literally on borrowed time, feeding on a very old story. Your institutions will continue to falter for the gift that you now hold within you does not recognize duality as being real. Such is the power of Christ consciousness. Collectively you hold the future of humanity in your heart. As the structures that have supported this dualistic game continue to grasp for air, yesterday will call and demand that you plan for your own survival. It will suggest that you hide out, store foods and wait for the tide to turn. We ask each of you, where is your joy? This transition need not be traumatic. Some of you will serve thousands directly as speakers, healers and teachers while others will serve thousands indirectly in your local neighborhoods and communities. All of you and all of your skills are needed. Not because the world is ending. You are the "lovers of life," you enjoy participating in the creation of anything that honors the sacredness of life. We want to remind you that the integrity of our relationship with each of you is based on mutual respect. We will not undermine that relationship by playing the role of a parent with up to the minute reports from our angelic newsroom. We gladly share our perspective and will continue to blend our presence with those who have placed their allegiance with their hearts. Life is good - breathe it in each and every moment.

Chapter Five

Burning the Inertia

Once again it is our pleasure to blend our presence with our physical counterparts. We want to remind each of you that perhaps you feel drawn to these words, this message, because you believe we have something to share that you are lacking. Perhaps you are looking for a deeper understanding of who you are and why you feel the way you do during this time of transition. It continues to be our joy to share with you how we perceive your reality but our intention is not to only deliver a message. Each and every time you desire to deepen your connection with the dynamic presence of your soul nature, we respond. It might be through these words but more often than not our presence can easily blend with the elements of nature or Gaia. It is here that we can caress your checks with the soft breeze of the wind or ignite your passion with bolts of lightening, help to cool your frustrations with the dampening rain and perhaps broaden your vision of your own magnificence whenever you acknowledge the beauty of this Earth.

Humanity is now just beginning to add another aspect to these elements, the ethers or our nonphysical reality. No matter how our relationship with you unfolds, it is always with one thought in mind. We miss you! We love you beyond any love that you have experienced as a human being.

We admire your courage to step into a physical reality with such enthusiasm. We serve you now to remind you of that. We adore you for your understanding that all of life is continuously changing and growing. We serve you now by reminding you of that. We admire your capacity to accept who you are at this moment. We serve you now by reminding you of this. Our relationship with you continues to evolve into a deep, mutual respect for each other. We understand that you have forgotten much of what you have always been while playing the role of a human being. We want you to understand that you are indeed perfect just as you are, complete and whole, and you are always changing. As you read these words, for a brief moment we have your attention. Can you not feel the immense love that these words often fail to translate? This is and will always be our most important message. We cannot help but love you for we are YOU!

Desiring Change

We understand your dilemma as a human being. Change on Earth seems to move like a turtle basking in the sun. Your belief in your natural abilities to create change has taken a beating every time you don't experience the change you desire for yourself or for this planet. It is our joy to remind you over and over again of your inherent abilities, not by judging or belittling you, for would you not agree that you have mastered that feat. Our love for you invites you to experience the many expressions of love. For we have spent the last 10 years with our partner (Robert) inviting you to embrace your human nature/ personality/ego. Our partner's personality believes these messages come from a separate identity and calls it channeling. His soul knows that we represent his lineage by speaking our truth, and that truth is that your soul is not a singular being. Our truth is that your human nature will never be able to perceive the bigger picture. Our teaching invites you to stop asking your human nature to guide your life.

The nature of embracing acknowledges and respects the existence of life as it is at this moment. Your human nature has been suffering from a broken heart for most of your life. It does not trust love for it only knows a love that has been consistently withdrawn. Healing the wounded heart of your human nature is essential. Your personality must learn to trust. Stop resisting in order to experience the immense presence of love from your own soul nature. Many of you attend spiritual gatherings simply to feel this new love, and this is very much a part of the healing process. The love that we have been sharing with many of you has resounded to the word-yes! Yes to life, yes to healing the pain of your past, yes to your ability to reclaim your birthright. Yes to self empowerment. Yes has such a beautiful resonance, do you not agree? By proclaiming, yes - you have also invited a non-dualistic relationship with another aspect of love.

Shining the Light

Prior to your incarnation, we sat together in council pondering the many choices each of you would consider. Together we would turn our attention to Earth and could easily perceive the energy fields of humanity. Do you re-member? Do you recall how we responded when we perceived the collective flickers of light representing a very diminished consciousness? Do you remember how we would respond when a human being awakened from their slumber and began to radiate such a powerful wave of en-ergy? Such a beautiful sight! Do you remember seeing how this radiance weaves its way into families, communities and entire countries? Do you recall our enthusiasm for en-visioning your life filled with this same potential?Acting as a beacon to transmit energies from the source within all of life. Placing yourselves in strategic locations so that your presence could impact your immediate environment. If you were to die today, you too would see a very different land-scape of energies now playing on Earth. For there are now millions of these beacons whose radiance extends, at times, several miles beyond their body.

It is indeed a great honor to hold yourself like a beacon for the Christ seed within you. This seed continues to grow and expand, and as it does, many of you are feeling unsettled and somewhat confused. Your radiance has evolved into an energy that now moves in and around all of life. The beacon continues to serve its purpose and many have been called or will continue to respond to the role of a transmitter of energy. This energy is, and will continue to, disrupt patterns of behavior that support a life that feels disconnected from Spirit. Although this might be very good news to many of you, it is not to many others. For they have grown addicted to the roles they are playing. As these vibrant new streams of energy continue to flow into and around all of life on Earth, many of your institutions will not be able to "flow" with the change that is required to adapt to this new frequency. We know that this too is very good news for many of you. For you desire to be a part of this change.

This love that now radiates through your bodies does not resonate with the love that your human nature understands. Nor is it content with simply destroying systems that do not align themselves with this potent consciousness. The very change that many of you desired to experience on Earth is shaking the foundations of many of your institutions that have provided a support for many and act as a type of control.

Again, we deeply honor your service as these beacons for life force energy. But at some point, as you feel these dated structures begin to dissolve, can you also feel the impulse from this very consciousness that you are serving to also create the new systems? You have done your job very well. And yet, do you not feel a restless presence growing within your solar plexus. For alongside all that will not withstand the changes MUST come the new creations. Many of you are feeling called to move and to now work with others who share your vision. Bringing your thoughts and ideas into a new collective, whether that be your immediate family, work place, community, or global enterprises. The very nature of the energy you have been serving is to create life. You have awakened the Christ seed within you and it has grown with you over the years. Its nature does not resonate with the majority of humanity at this time. It does however resonate with many of you and is inviting you to develop a conscious relationship with your co-creative abilities.

Many of you have enjoyed a somewhat quiet, simple life. Such a life served your service as the beacon. As the Christ seed continues to grow, many of you are feeling frustrated that so many of your old habits or desires no longer bring you the same satisfaction. You recommit yourself to being a more focused beacon only to discover this now lacks the same joy or passion. This can be frustrating and at times very confusing for you feel this immense energy flowing through you and at the same time your life feels somewhat empty. The Christ seed cannot be contained within the parameters of your past. If your desire is to be of service to this very potent consciousness, now would be an excellent time to embrace your immense abilities as a creator.

The Law of Attraction

Our service to you is to remind you again of the incredible service you have and continue to offer to all of life, including Earth. You have changed the play on Earth, and perhaps now would be a good time to revisit the dressing room and to claim your role as an active and conscious creator. You will find at this time there is much attention being given to the "law of attraction." Those that played the role of a beacon and awakened the Christ seed now become the leaders for this consciousness. How does that feel, Beloveds? Leaders and teachers? The days of following outdated patterns of behavior will interfere with the gift that you carry within your heart and belly. This Christ seed is burning with a love for life that will carve its way into physical reality through your hands, hearts, and mind. Understanding the law of attraction can serve your relationship with the aspects within you that resist this transformation into unity consciousness. It is our joy to remind you of the nature of this law and its impact on your life. We also remind you that your planet has been gifted with the most comprehensive presentation of this law by the ones called Abraham/Hicks.

The gift that was granted to you long ago was the freedom to embody whatever state of consciousness you would choose for yourself. Again, we remind you that the state of consciousness that many of you already embody accepted this lifetime as an opportunity to serve something greater than your human self. You agreed to carry within you the very solution to this polarized reality. You also agreed to reflect back a living model of this Christ seed for others to perceive. You did not agree to compromise your own value or worth in the process of modeling this new consciousness. We talked about this relationship in our book (Riding a Stallion), and invite you to read those chapters again to refresh your passion. The law of attraction is very clear, the life force energies that support all of creation, what you call Spirit, will reflect back to each of you a mirror image of how you are feeling. How are you feeling Beloveds? May we assist you in reminding you how life, in this very moment, is waiting to serve you? We hear your frustrations each time you shout - why is life taking so long to reply?

Your Energetic Bank Account

Let's explore how life does serve you. Imagine that your body serves you as a personal energetic bank. This bank, your body, acts as a storehouse for living resources or Spirit. Much like your monetary banking systems, your body gives you daily reports that reflect the energetic status of your withdrawals and deposits of life force energy. You "read" these statements based on how you are feeling. This energy downloads into your personal account from life affirming choices that are supported by thoughts that reinforce the value you have placed on your own life. The physical well being of your body is dependent on a steady flow of energetic deposits. The magnetic quality of your body attracts to it energies that are aligned with the status of your bank account. Building a healthy storehouse of energetic deposits in your body greatly amplifies your radiance and your creative abilities.

The art of "being in receivership" is another way of giving yourself permission to step into the flow of accepting free life force energy. When you shout out to the universe with all of your heart that you desire more money, better jobs or a compatible lover or friend, we want you to know that your thoughts are heard. We also want you to develop a better understanding of why your desires are not experienced.

As we have said many times, being in receivership can feel very vulnerable when you have been conditioned to shield yourself from life. These shields literally block the presence of Spirit from coming into your body, your life.

Being in receivership of life affirming energies is a very potent deposit. It supports the health and well being of new cells in your body that are capable of supporting the immense presence of Christ consciousness. Being conscious of a continuous flow of deposits into your energetic bank account builds a very vibrant, magnetic presence. Such a presence makes it very easy for the universe to serve you.

Many of you opened yourself to feeling the presence of Spirit with great enthusiasm. What you didn't expect to experience was an intense period of physical detox. The discomfort from feeling the withdrawal symptoms created yet another polarized relationship with Spirit. Receiving the dynamic presence of Spirit is your gift to yourself. It is based on self love! The patterns of behavior you inherited support a state of consciousness that feels disconnected from Spirit. That separation gave birth to a "feeding frenzy"- feeding on anything that could act as a substitute for Spirit. As you have already discovered, you have lost your appetite for these substitutes. It is natural for your "cravings" to want to be fed, they are simply attempting to fulfill the void. A conscious devotion to a steady stream of deposits can radically shift your conditioned behaviors in just 30 days. Let yourself feel the anger and resentment and express that energy in any creative way you can imagine for yourself.

We want you to understand how your conditioning maintains a community of cells in your body that feed on conditioned patterns of behavior. These conditioned cells are literally withdrawing life supporting energies from your bank or body. They reflect the consciousness of your past that gave birth to your human nature or personality. Without your permission and on a daily basis this personality continues to play mental tapes from your past that in turn withdraw energies from your bank account, leaving some of you feeling exhausted or energetically bankrupt. Your energetic bank account acts like a magnet, attracting to it energies that match your personal balance statement.

Withdrawals are being made, on a daily basis from indulging in feelings of doubt, worry, and concern. Your personality's solution to this imbalance is to try to convince you that you must work harder, put more effort into achieving and pursuing its conditioned agenda, an agenda that is based on finding love outside of itself. If it fails to achieve its agenda, it becomes passive, disengages from life, withdrawing more energy from your bank account with feelings of remorse, self pity and disillusionment. How then does love serve you by saying no? If you discovered that someone had withdrawn from your monetary bank account most of your savings or investments without your permission, would your response be to embrace them? Pat them on the back? If one of your own children or friends was withdrawing funds from your personal bank account on a daily basis without your permission, would you truly feel like giving them a hug? We want to be very clear about this for indeed, on a daily basis and without your permission, the conditioned thoughts that continue to play in your head over and over again are withdrawing life supporting energies from your own energetic bank account. Over time, these withdrawls of energy from your bank or body greatly diminish your body's ability to act as a powerful magnet for your heart's desires. Sacrificing your joy in the consciousness that you have invited into your life becomes a major withdrawal. Deposits into your energetic bank account are based on self love, self nurturance and self fulfillment placing YOU at the very front of your life to now receive your true worth.

Being Passive

Earth or Gaia has an agreement with all of life. Any being or consciousness is welcome to be here on one condition, it must take a body. She allows all of life, no matter its consciousness to experience itself in flesh. You are surrounded by a consciousness that has forgotten that all of life is sacred and will forever expand. Coexisting with this consciousness or the collective energy of your conditioned beliefs has stretched the patience of even the saints among you. We are suggesting that your patience is being misplaced at this time. For those of you that have been embracing this little puppy, your ego, we bow before your patience. We understand the hypnotic qualities of physical reality and how easy it is to become passive about your choices.

Now is the time to become consciously accountable to your own creations. We desire that this become a joyful experience and not be used as another opportunity to beat yourself up. A very potent way to address the issue of withdrawals and deposits is to keep a journal of your days activities. At the end of each day, be honest about how you were feeling. Notice if there is a pattern in some of your activities, and if so, can you gift yourself by changing how you are feeling. It might not be necessary to change your activity but you can change, at any moment how you feel. Try it right now. Simply take a deep breathe, exhale and notice at the end of your exhale that there exists a slight difference from how you felt just a moment ago. Turn your attention to this slight difference and observe how it begins to grow and eventually becomes your preference.

Life affirming choices leave you feeling enthusiastic, joyful, courageous and at times blissful to name but a few. When you notice these thoughts running in your head that leave you feeling depressed, confused or disillusioned, take a deep breath and imagine feeling anything that is slightly different. You don't jump from depression to bliss in one breath. But if your attention is on allowing a steady flow of deposits into your energetic bank account, in time bliss will kiss your cheeks. The conditioned thoughts that support your human nature are literally withdrawing your most precious life resource - Spirit, without your permission! Without the presence of Spirit, not only does your own health suffer, but the very presence of your own soul is not compatible with an environment that lacks the life force to support it. Have you not noticed that we venture for only short periods of time into your reality? The universe responds to your desires by reading your personal bank account. By the law of attraction, it will respond to your desire and match it based on your current balance statement. You can change that statement to become whatever you desire. As you build an abundant, energetic bank account within you, your body acts as a powerful magnet to draw to it whatever your heart desires. What does your heart desire? Have these desires been lying dormant, waiting for your imagination to give them life? Have you noticed how boring it has become to allow your human nature to continue to play the victim leaving you feeling impoverished on so many levels.

There exist many teachings and practices that have been designed to awaken and help maintain the presence of Spirit in your body. As well, the choices you make for yourself that encourage you to love yourself as you have never loved yourself before are very potent deposits that the universe MUST reflect back. Maintaining a healthy, balanced inner bank account puts the universe at your feet. You designed it to serve you. It is more than a hope or a dream, it offers itself as an energetic partner. Keeping a journal is a powerful tool to help you become conscious of your daily withdraws and deposits.

Many of you desire to feel the immense presence of your soul and yet your body or energetic bank account is lacking the deposits to support such a magnificent presence. You have already demonstrated your patience with your personality, self love now says "No." No more withdrawals. For these withdrawals diminish your ability to truly enjoy your life. If you are willing to engage in this simple but powerful exercise for the next 30 days, you will discover that you can choose how you want to feel, and how you are feeling will define your experience. Allowing the dynamic, multidimensional presence of your soul to literally descend into every cell of your body brings to you the support for ALL of your heart's desires. You have invoked the presence of Christ consciousness into your life.

Its potency can be overwhelming to your human nature. The personality will want to continue to withdraw from life for it knows it is not qualified to work with this energy. It is time, personality, to surrender to the presence that is qualified to embody the Christ - for it knows, your soul, THAT IT IS THE CHRIST!

We come full circle then with the ones who acted as beacons for an energy that has disrupted the collective consciousness of humanity. This energy now seeks expression, movement, and expansion. You cannot contain the very nature of life. It won't feel safe if you attempt to control it. It will feel destructive. Look closely at the thoughts that seem to passively play out in your mind and yet dominate your perception. Don't take our word for it. Stop thinking for 10 minutes and then share with us how you feel. Indeed, choose life by choosing how you want to feel by choosing how you want to think about how you want to perceive your life. The magnetic presence of the collective consciousness of humanity is supported by thoughts that radiate out, for ALL to hear. Thoughts that suggest you are less than source energy. Stop listening to these. You agreed to experience the pain of humanities consciousness, that part of your life is complete. You also agreed to model the very solution to that inner conflict. This part of your life is waiting to support you with tremendous joy and passion.

The creators have awakened. It is time to celebrate a truly fulfilling life. Place yourself at the front of life and receive ALL that your heart now desires!

Chapter Six

Sex, Money and Power

transcribed and edited from a live channeled session

It is with great joy that we blend our presence with your reality and to share our perspective about this wonderful year called 2008. It was four years ago that we mentioned this year as having the potential to inspire great change. As with all potentials, timing is very important. This is the year however that you can finally - finally feel "turned-on" by life. The potentials for this year fill our hearts with such joy as we acknowledge how difficult life on Earth has been for each of you. Many of you have been asking, when, if ever, is my life going to change? When will I experience the bliss that others speak of? When will I receive the abundance that has been promised? When will I feel the unlimited nature of my soul? Indeed, we suggest you buckle your seat belts and prepare yourself for the ride of your life!

We have spoken of how you changed your destiny in 1987 by declaring a new love for self. This was a pivotal time of choice for your planet. If that choice had not been made, it is very unlikely that any of you would still be here. So we say to you again and again, thank you!

The year of 1991 offered another choice. You were asked if you would be willing to allow your soul nature or higher self to coexist with your human nature. Once again you responded with a resounding yes even though your mind doesn't recall ever being asked the question. None of you realized how challenging this new relationship would be for your personality. Your human nature has been conditioned to rely on the mind to support its identity. Your soul nature uses its imagination to generate feelings that ignite creative potentials. The creative abilities of your soul reside in your heart and become activated by your feelings. For this new relationship to flourish, your personality and your mind can no longer control your perceptions. They must be willing to serve your consciousness. How is that going beloveds? Did we bite off more than we can chew? Indeed, now you know why many stepped aside when you offered to incarnate during this lifetime! For the last 17 years, most of you have been involved with healing the wounded heart of your human nature. You have learned to feel the energetic presence of your soul and you are learning to integrate that relationship into your day-to-day reality.

Of late, many of you have experienced a pause in your life. You felt that you had somehow taken a few steps back in your spiritual growth. Some of you even felt that your soul had abandoned you. We can assure you your soul is right here. This pause is here to serve you. This is a pause that has you acknowledging the state of your relationship between your human nature and your soul.

We remind you that your soul nature is willing to assume complete responsibility for your life and accepts all the conditions of your past. This pause represents another pivotal moment in your life to choose. It gives your human nature time to reflect upon its control issues for it feels bored. All of the concerns, worries and doubts that reside in your mind are draining the precious life resources from your physical vessel. Now, for most of humanity this is an ongoing, unconscious relationship that keeps your hospitals fully staffed. You are at a very different crossroad. The year 2008 offers itself as another opportunity to choose again. No matter where you are at with your life, the choices you make this year that honor the inherent integrity of your own soul nature will unleash a wave of passion unlike anything you have experienced before. We remind you, life is here to serve YOU. Most of you have requested a life that is filled with joy, passion and good health. Many of you have also denied yourself an authentic relationship with joy by processing the collective energy of humanity. You have used this relationship with these collective energies to deny yourself a sovereign connection with source. You deny yourself your birthright by denying yourself self love in order not to expose yourself as being truly magnificent. Your mind insists you can sidetrack this whole teacher business by downloading into your body the collective turmoil of humanity.

During this time of reflection there exists the opportunity to taste a freedom unlike anything you have ever experienced before as a human being. We are here, once again to ask you to make another choice. Are you willing to now surrender your control of life and place your trust in your soul nature? During the last 17 years, has it earned that trust? The choice that now lies before you is very potent. It will ignite your creative abilities and awaken your second chakra. This sacred seal is ready to serve you, and as it does, you will be gifted with the opportunity to acknowledge your relationship to "sex, money and power." It is time to truly honor self! Your mind insists it represents that self. To honor self, you must choose if you are ready to allow your consciousness or soul nature to represent you.

We have been teaching your human nature how to disengage energetically from dysfunctional relationships that support a feeling of being disconnected from joy. Disconnected from passion. Disconnected from love. Like any addiction, it takes time to change patterns of behavior that rely on others giving to you what you are unwilling to give to yourself. Indeed, this dance of victimhood upon planet earth is very intoxicating. This year, 2008, offers so many new potentials, that will invite you to become very honest about how you are feeling. This pause is a gift. For many of you are feeling no life at all. It is a void for you to consider a new choice that supports your magnificence. Life awaits your choice and will respond during the first part of this new year with a feeling that life is again moving, changing and expanding. That choice will invite you to have a conscious relationship with how you feel about sex, money and power. Potent energies that reside within your second chakra. Lets explore those issues and offer some insights that we believe can serve you.

Money

We would say that 2008 is all about freeing your creative abilities. What would you need to change in your life for you to truly experience an unlimited flow of abundance? Are you willing to joyfully befriend "money" as a valid and vital part of your own wellbeing?

Many of you relate to money like an unwanted guest. You tolerate its presence, but for the most part you see it as an obstacle to your own freedom. You see how money is so often used to reinforce a deluded sense of personal power. That delusion is equally represented whether there is a lack of abundance of money. In this new relationship with your soul nature, money serves YOU. Money has no power over your choices, it freely serves your new passion for living. Many of you refuse to trust that having money in your life can enrich your relationship with Spirit. This is the year to honestly look at how each of you are reacting to conditioned beliefs that deny you your true freedom. Money is a neutral energy until you infuse it with your own thoughts and emotions. In this new relationship with your soul nature, how can money serve you? Let's play with that question.

To change your relationship with anything you must be willing to change how you are "feeling." We know there is great joy in wanting to intellectually change your beliefs without having to address how you are feeling. From our perspective, your world would be be vibrating to a very different energy if that approach was effective. Money only knows how to play one game-follow the leader. We want to introduce some ideas for you to consider or practice that will ensure that money is following you.

Let's begin with how you support your physical vessel. In this new relationship we are inviting you to feel really "turned-on" by life. How could you make your food shopping experience more fulfilling? Buying food for yourself is a direct, physical relationship with self love. Many of you experience shopping for food to be a chore or obligation. How could it become something you really look forward to? The next time you go shopping, double the amount of time you give yourself and be willing to indulge all of your senses. As you scan the fruits and vegetables, take time to touch the texture, smell the flavors and enjoy the array of colors. These foods will also be blending and merging with your life. Most of you allow yourself to feel great joy while you anticipate hearing a channeled message. Are you willing to play with those feelings as they relate to your food?

Shopping for food can become a full body, orgasmic relationship if you are willing to change how you feel about that experience. When it's time to pay for the food, stay connected to those feelings of joy and gratitude. As you reach for your money, it too offers itself to blend and merge with your life. Appreciate that relationship. Let yourself get excited about the potentials.

Once a month each of you also place a great deal of energy on paying your bills. It is rare to find someone who enjoys that experience. This however is a perfect opportunity to shift your "feelings" and empower yourself. Can bill paying become a spiritual ritual that is infused with life affirming thoughts? Are you willing to play with the power of your feelings? Using the shopping experience as an example, sit before your pile of bills, face the envelopes and allow yourself the freedom to feel a sincere sense of gratitude for the services that have been provided. Look at each envelope or bill as a gift. Slowly unwrap it. Feel its sharp edges, admire the color of the paper and caress the texture of the bill. Appreciate, appreciate and appreciate again the opportunity to dance with life as you now thank those that supported your desire to have a home, heat, clothes and water. Let yourself go deeply into feeling a sense of gratitude as you write your checks. Lick the envelopes with joy, and place them in your mailbox acknowledging how good it feels when "money" serves you. It must. Money has no choice. In this new relationship with your soul nature, you must choose for yourself how YOU want to feel. The pause that so many of you are experiencing is to be honored. Your personality is exhausted and is using this time to reflect upon the nature of your soul. Play with "feeling" different in all the ways money plays a part in your life. Watch how a part of you is very invested in pretending that you follow money. As if money doesn't deserve to have an intimate relationship with you. This is powerful co-creation at its best.

Personal Power

In this year of 2008, your sense of power or feeling powerless will ask of you to make a choice. The power that your mind seeks to obtain has a very fragile foundation. We believe you will begin to see this crumble within the collective consciousness of humanity this year. As this new year unfolds, the opportunity to reunite your human qualities with your angelic roots is ripe for change. You will find that our relationship is shifting to accommodate your growing awareness. We speak often of being your physical counterparts, and for the most part you can accept that intellectually. 2008 invites you to embody our relationship, shift your identity and begin to speak and act from this new perspective. Channeling, as you understand this type of communication is also changing. Those who allow us to blend or meld our consciousness with their human identity will flourish if the human part takes responsibility for also embodying that presence. We have shared many times that it is our intention to work and play alongside the human being. We offer ourselves in relationship with your humanness, speaking alongside your conditioned beliefs. The separation that has existed for eons between our realities has shifted, inviting you to consciously participate in a re-unification of all of your counterparts. To your singular human nature this feels like a corporate takeover. It will need time to adjust to your true muliti-dimensional nature as it blends and merges with your human experience.

Personal power as it relates to your mind becomes an illusion. Your new sense of power is reinforced by the actions you take to ensure that YOUR life is fulfilling, rewarding and reconnected with source. This year is your time to claim your truth. A time to stop listening to the lies of your mind and begin to imagine just new opportunities for yourself. Your personal power reflects your ability and willingness to love yourself. Trusting that you are worthy of having a grand galactic family and its presence living alongside you in this physical reality. Trusting that your body knows how to accommodate this new relationship if you would stop listening to your minds agenda. Your personal power finally emerges when you experience the bliss of a mind that has learned to serve your consciousness. A profound sense of peace is waiting for you.

2008 offers this magnificent choice. This new relationship cannot be simulated. There is no substitution for it and very few living models. It is not supported by following the words of others, no matter how inspired you might feel. It supports itself each and every time you claim your own unique truth and recognize how vital that is to the "whole."

This year you will understand that compromising your own sense of power or wellbeing is a form of self denial. Denying yourself love. As you place yourself in the front of the line of life to receive your true worth, you will need to embrace your personality's reluctance to accept such a gift. Embrace how it has learned to support itself by feeling unworthy. As you begin to feel a new passion for life, acknowledge the conditions that would deny such a feeling but claim these new feelings as your own truth. Is it your truth to be shy? It is your truth to lack an abundance of resources? Is it your truth that you missed the boat that is heading towards personal enlightenment because of your age? You must claim how YOU want to feel and then act on these "new" feelings. Energy in motion will solidify and integrate your relationship with your soul. Again, don't take our word for it. Put this new relationship to the test. If the nature of your soul is truly unlimited, dump your entire history at its feet and witness its reaction. If your soul is capable of embodying unconditional love, take that love for a test drive. Let it drive your life and see if it is trustworthy, competent and reliable.

Sexuality

2008 is all about beginning to feel "turned-on" by life. Which naturally leads us to your relationship with the most sacred energy within you. Your creative life force or your sexuality. Your sexuality reminds you that life is also about pleasure, joy, bliss and ecstasy. Your human nature is conditioned to relate to your sexual desires from a place of guilt and shame. Very few have been taught how to use sexual feelings as a way to reconnect with source energy. Your sexuality is not limited to your sexual organs. It is but a focal point of pleasure that invites you to circulate these ecstatic energies to every part of your body. To every part of your life.

This year invites you to reconnect your life with orgasmic waves of pleasure. You already know how to imagine that for yourself sexually. Imagine playing with those feelings in other areas of your life. Feeling turned on by life connects you with source energy. Sharing that energy with those aspects of yourself that feel disconnected offers a very new relationship. You are changing the dynamics between the polarized aspects of what you term light and dark. Your soul and personality represent symbolic aspects of a galactic dilemma.

Feeling turned on by life opens the floodgates of joy. Let these new passions flow, with your mind acting as a witness. The passions don't try to overwhelm the fear with their presence. They will wash over the doubts and concerns like a river over rocks knowing that it is futile to resist such a love. It is only a matter of time before the rock eventually moves, but that time also ends up being your experience of life. As you play with your sexual passions or your creative life force energies, let the energy circulate up your spine and down your body over and over again. You will develop a newfound freedom to express your joy for life. In this year 2008, you will also discover that this joy cannot be held in place. It cannot be contained within the safety of your conditioned past. Your mind isn't qualified to represent your magnificence, it is qualified to support it. Your mind is not qualified to be the new teacher in this new relationship. Those of you that step forward will experience the fears of your mind and the bliss of your soul. Initially, the dance between these aspects won't appear very graceful or professional to your human pride. It is not about how well you dance but whether you are you willing to do this dance. It is that time!

Personal power has nothing to do with perfecting yourself. In this new relationship, your soul accepts all the fears you inherited and it still acts on its own desires. It accepts that your personality will most likely complain at every new turn you make in your life. It accepts that, but it doesn't allow those fears to stop it from acting. In time, perhaps during your entire lifetime, your personality might learn to trust in the integrity of your soul nature. Not because you visualize such a relationship in the safety of your meditations. This trust is solely based on your willingness to act on your heart's desires, even when your knees feel weak, your throat becomes dry or your solar plexus has turned into a knot. Your soul accepts all of that and gently whispers to your mind - you are not responsible for my life. Relax and let us do this together.

Claiming how you want to feel leaves no one else to blame. This kind of freedom is not for everyone. Many will continue to be fed by whatever story exists in the past that puts others in charge of their current dilemma. I, Michael, have not hidden from you the turmoils that do exist in the stars or your freedom to discover your own unique place in creation. This year offers such a profound opportunity to develop a first-hand relationship with source energy as it exists within your soul nature. Sex, money and power sit like pillars in your life waiting for your imagination to set them free to now serve you.

Our love for you is beyond your knowing. Be fore-warned, we are not shy about our feelings for each of you.

Michael refers to the year 2008 throughout this entire message but I also believe it is timeless.

Chapter Seven

New Opportunties

So, indeed this is a very potent time to be on your planet. This is a potent time for each of you. Before you incarnated, we spoke of these times as being a profound opportunity to give birth to a new consciousness, a new relationship to the energy of a human being. You were well aware of the challenges on our side of the veil and now that you are in the thick of it, you sometimes wonder why you ever choose to volunteer for such a experience.

This work to change your identity is challenging. Extremely challenging. All of you have played with this relationship in other lifetimes. You found it impossible to give your devotion to this energy and still participate in your day-to-day world. Many of you here are some of the more renowned nuns and shamans, priests and priestesses. Your new sanctuary or monastery is now very mobile, it travels with you wherever you go and acts as a beacon for your own consciousness. Of course we are speaking for your sacred temple - the body.

Each of you discovered that your human nature is connected to the collective consciousness of all of humanity and is very much addicted, very much entrenched in the conditions and parameters that you inherited. You conformed to these conditioned beliefs simply to be accepted, to fit in as best you could to this collective consciousness. Now you are finding that these very conditions are interfering with your ability to embody your soul and Christ consciousness.

We have watched all of you in this last year play with this new relationship. Finding that not everyone resonates to what you are doing. Not everyone fully understands or even appreciates what it is that you are willing to embody. Not just intellectually embrace some new concepts. But to fully embody the living presence of the Christ. Tasting a profound state of joy, ecstasy and bliss. Very few humans have truly experienced such a connection with life.

The changes that you are feeling in your body, on this planet, these changes that you are experiencing in your personal life, you are at the very crest of a very powerful cycle affecting all of life on Earth. We would say that the crest of this energy that is making itself available to all of you is offering an opportunity to surrender to the energy of a new passion that is supported by the sacred feminine, the divine mother. This is the lifetime to be in receivership.

And so it is that all of you are feeling in your own lives all the places that you resist this change, and we know for many of you this has grown to be rather irritating and humorous, indeed. It allows you to have an experience with this energy called victimhood. The energy of victimhood is a waning identity that no longer serves you, and yet you feel you are also saying goodbye to an old trusted friend. Here we find many of you hesitating, for you have grown so accustomed to playing the victim and yet your soul nature grows restless. The passion stirs and you begin to remember the value of self empowerment.

This cycle of energy is asking and inviting each of you, will you take the reins of this new passion and create with it in your life? Or will you choose to procrastinate and find reasons for why it feels uncomfortable to be on top of this passion- uncomfortable owning your own creative abilities. This cycle of energy that is here to serve you serves your intention to stop following and start leading. For as we approach the grand marker of time, 2012, humanity will need new leaders and teachers that can guide those that are questioning a life that is out of balance.

Is there time in your life to receive the presence of your soul nature that your heart has yearned to feel? Are you willing to devote some quality time to practice being in receivership of the presence of your own heritage – the Heart of Creation? Choosing this presence can be the foundation that supports your emerging identity- one that becomes as real as you are willing to "feel" it.

You see it is not as hard as you thought it would be. Is it truly all about enjoying life? Coming together as friends, neighbors, community and serving this emerging presence. Is there joy in serving joy? Put it to the test. Let your self fully engage in such a service but not from the old way of needing to compromise your own sense of joy. How would you experiment with complimenting and enhancing the presence of the Heart of Creation?

The most courageous of you have asked; if my new identity is not based on the roles that I am playing now, then who would I be? If I let the presence of this living love infiltrate into my parenting, friendships and workplace,

74

would I taste this joy? And we say to all of you-indeed! But if the role you are playing won't allow this presence to be a part of your life, don't beat yourself up. Just stop playing the role for awhile and see what happens.

This ride is not for everyone. Only a few are willing to truly embrace this type of freedom. It asks of you to maintain a conscious connection with Source energy so as to facilitate that presence, this living love that is supporting all of life and calling it You. Unity consciousness becomes your new identity.

We will remind you that the presence of love that reflects source energy has not been witnessed by many human beings. There have been very few models and of the few that allowed this presence in their life, your institutions tampered with their truth. We indeed understand your hesitation and your dilemma. And yet the yearning in your heart persists. It wants to feel and see its own reflection through your eyes. It is not your problem if humanity has a problem with the presence of source energy making itself known through you - as YOU!

So, here we are at the apex of one of the most powerful energies to ever enter your Earth, and we see your bodies saying how do I integrate this, and it cannot if you keep playing ping pong with your sense of devotion.

There is much conflict within you that all gets resolved if you just devote yourself to being in the presence of this living love who will support and resolve your inner turmoil. It seems too simple to be true. But again, don't take our word for it, put it to the test. How many ways are you willing to experience this presence and maintain that connection. We have seen for many of you that when you do reconnect, a sense of clarity comes to your mind. As if to say, beloved soul, as your mind I no longer want to be responsible for trying to figure out how to be spiritual. I have been working overtime with my divine, finite perception. I have been pursuing and trying to achieve spiritual accomplishments for a long time. Our body is clearly stating that we have accomplished feeling exhausted. Your minds, beloved are waiting for its counterpart, this living love, its divine lover the Heart of Creation.

The presence of God/Goddess itself is that powerful. Without any effort on your part, allow her to now be the foundation for your new identity. We invited you to practice 3 times a day for 30 minutes being in her presence. To feel how it is that you resist being loved by life because you have been taught as a human being that love equals pain. You were lied to.

You are beginning to sense that the only truth that truly supports who you are becoming resides within this presence of energy. Some of you are experiencing a profound state of contentment and bliss that encourages you to trust more and more in the validity of this presence supporting your life. You will begin to trust in your creative abilities as they respond to this energy, inspiring you to now create a life that is very fulfilling.

Your new dilemma will be your relationship with your conditioned human nature. How does the unlimited nature of your soul dance with so many fears and limitations? We invite you to take a moment to breath here. Take a moment to honor the personality that has upheld this energy of victimhood. It has done its very best to support that intention to play victimized. Take a moment to say to this personality, this ego, I, soul, am truly here now. Thank you Beloved friend for serving my life, and now let me serve you. Let me serve you. Feel the presence of this love that you have practiced allowing to flow into your life. You are not to blame. No one is to blame. I, soul choose to have a healthy relationship now. A conscious relationship with you. I invite you, ego, to be my inner lover such is my devotion now to the new role that you will play in my life. It is a role that does not ask of you to take responsibility for my humanness any longer. I devote myself to reestablishing the trust that I will not abandon you ego. I will demonstrate my devotion to being fully present in this body by consciously sharing this presence of living love with you - ego. Such is my respect for the job you assumed but were not qualified to do.

This new relationship will take some time. All of you unsuccessfully have attempted to intellectually love the ego, to intellectually love those aspects of yourself that embarrass you. You discovered it did not work. But something else does work. You developed an emotional relationship with your personality and it developed trust.

In this new relationship, self fulfillment is not ego gratification. A fulfilled human being allows the living presence of love to support itself and freely shares the overflow of that love with all of life, including your conditioned human nature. This doesn't mean that you must pamper your ego, the presence of this love is very dynamic and its relationship with your conditioned past might at times be best described as "tough love." We deeply honor each of you. Your personal freedom doesn't depend on you achieving anything. Your freedom asks of you, will you allow the living presence of love to infiltrate into your life and into every cell of your body?

Chapter Eight

Trust in Yourself

Trust, what a delightful invitation! Without "knowing" - is trusting trustworthy? Or must the mind intervene, filter the invitation, and distort the potentials. In this moment there is a deep, penetrating silence that is being shared alongside these words as a presence or a consciousness that is fully self aware. It does not need to be defined for it to know itself. It exists before thought. Can the mind trust such a relationship and allow it to unfold, touching every fiber of your being? It is challenging for the human to imagine that your existence is not dependent upon a description. Thought plays a vital role in this immense, cosmic relationship. It serves this silence by creating a focus to reflect upon. This unlimited aspect of you dwells within the silence of all of creation and invites you, through trusting, to feel its presence. As the intensity of the expansion of consciousness on Earth continues to impact every area of your life, each of you stand upon a simple yet profound foundation - Trust. A foundation that will serve to awaken your true identity. Trusting in life as you have never allowed yourself to trust before. This is profound beloved human.

It is our joy to deepen our relationship with each of you and to remind you that humanity is very fortunate to have you here at this time. Without your presence, it does not appear to us that humanity has the capacity to resolve their dilemma. We understand that for the most part humanity has not shared their appreciation for the work that you do. For most of your lives you have, and will continue to rely on, a level of support that comes from small groups, channeled messages and relationships that support themselves from honest, direct communication. You have heard us say through our partner and others many times that we, your nonphysical counterparts, kiss your feet every moment of every day. We kiss your feet to show our gratitude for your service to the "whole."

Your willingness and desire to come to Earth has allowed you to explore the most delicious and immediate reflection of your own thoughts and emotions. For many of you, that desire is just beginning to become realized as you disentangle yourself from all the conditioning that you also volunteered to experience. You are just beginning to taste the wonders of how life wants to serve you. Life waits for everyone but the time is ripe to now act on your emerging passion. A passion that for many of you exists in your imagination, waiting to reveal itself in all of your relationships. It requires tremendous trust on your part. Acting without knowing that it is real. We hear many of you suggest that it is easy for us to proclaim these truths in a environment that so easily supports our passions. Again, we are not the ones that stepped up to the front of the line and declared ourselves more qualified to serve the "whole" in this lifetime - to demonstrate, firsthand, how to heal the pain of experiencing a love withheld and to live free of many of the parameters that reside within the human mind. You tasted and endured the human condition. NOW it is time for humanity to taste your divine condition. It is time for your soul nature to have its way with physical reality. It is time to call forth and allow the presence that supports all of life to now reconnect to your own life and to put it to work. It is time for your divine presence to reclaim ownership of these vessels you call bodies, to ignite the Christ seed within every cell and begin to radiate a profound joy for being alive. Within the human condition there is so much that denies you this expression. We understand your dilemma but we know, even if you have forgotten who we are speaking too.

You did not come here to offer "the" map to Spirit. Humanity's history is filled with stories of battles over who has the "best" map to God. We see so many humans infatuated with the need to be right by making others wrong. Alongside that depressing spiral is a fragile new beginning held in place by such a powerful presence called trust. You are the new map makers of reality that have the potential to become guides rather than commandments for an emerging consciousness that is based on self love.

We understand how you were encouraged to swallow a set of beliefs that never truly resonated with you. A belief that you would need to compete for love. A belief that God/Goddess resided outside of you. A belief that this higher power would grant you your desires if you demonstrated that you are worthy, in God's eyes, to receive such a gift. You were told that your angelic counterparts would bring to you what you need in life. You agreed to at least appear to entertain these beliefs until a time came for you to reveal your true identity. That time is NOW!

82

We understand and have great compassion for how you endured these painful lies in order to survive. It comes as no surprise to any of us that you have also entertained a desire to get off of this planet, a planet that supports itself with much of what you know to be untrue. Many of you began to realize that these channeled messages where simply reflecting back to you your own inner truth. You began to awaken from the pain of your human experience that denied you "feeling" the presence of your own soul nature. For some of you, this presence has been known to you for many years, and yet you still find yourself lacking what your heart truly desires. You began to wonder if we are simply dangling a carrot in front of you but never really delivering the goods. You have been promised a more fulfilled life that is overflowing with new potentials, health and great sex. Many of you have cried out to the heavens above demanding proof that these new potentials show themselves as being real. You demanded to see YOUR truth reflected upon this stage called Earth. You feel that without this connection life has no purpose.

Unlike us, you taste firsthand all of the lies and deceptions played out in front of you on a daily basis. So we say to you again that this is but the beginning of a grand potential for change. Life cannot choose for you, but it must, without choice, reflect back to you whatever you choose for yourself. You are at the front line of a new cycle that will introduce a new consciousness to humanity. You now carry all the support you require within yourself. The Christ seed becomes activated each and every time you allow the presence or energy of your soul nature to coexist with your human condition. Your soul nature again looks at all aspects of your life and proclaims - "I'm okay with all of it. May I coexist within this story you have created or must I be another out-of-body experience?" Surrendering to this presence resolves the conflict you inherited that insisted that you must compete for love. Many of you have discovered that love itself has no agenda. It finds you extraordinarily beautiful just as you are. Your soul finds your human condition irresistible. Don't take our word for it - simply allow the love that your soul has for you at this moment to penetrate every cell of your body. Your soul finds all of your perceived imperfections to be perfect!

On this day we ask then that our partner relax as he feels the presence that has always supported his identity. To remind each of you that we, your angelic counterparts, serve YOU. We understand that this grand story unfolding on Earth presents challenges on every level of your being. It is our truth that YOU carry the very solution to all the illusions that exist within this reality called Earth. We encourage you to shift your allegiance to the part of you that finds great joy in this adventure. It does not feel that this gift is a burden.

We have spoken of the Christ seed and of the lineage of those that carry this gift. We have asked you to begin to "feel" that your body acts like an energetic bank account. We have invited you to become more conscious and attentive to the ongoing deposits and withdrawls from your personal account. We remind you that taking responsibility for your own energetic affairs will allow you to taste the reflection of your own magnificence. We also see an obstacle that lies directly in front of each of you that is directly related to your human condition. Your ability to "trust" in life is very fragile.

Trust is a very potent virtue, for it overrides your personal history without regard to all of the agendas that support that past. We are not suggesting you throw out your discernment or common sense, but many of you have already tasted the presence of such an innocence that would trust life for no apparent reason. Many of you already have experienced an overwhelming sense of freedom simply by trusting in your inherent abilities without knowing what those are.

Let's explore this issue of trusting by acknowledging some of the ways you already trust that life will serve you very well. When you wake up in the morning, you don't give any thought to whether or not the sun will rise. You simply trust that it will. When you crawl out of bed, you take for granted that your body will stand, walk and begin to function just as you would like it too. You trust you won't swallow your toothbrush. You trust when you turn your water faucet on, it will flow each and every time. You trust that when you turn the ignition in your car, it will start the engine. You trust that when you swallow your food, the rest of your body knows what to do with it. You trust that when you fall and scrape your knee, your body has the ability to heal that wound. Some of you have studied how these beautiful bodies are so proficient at self repair while most of you simply take it for granted without knowing how it works. You, dear human already trust so many facets of life.

As a child, your desire to walk reinforced your trust in life when walking became trustworthy. Your desire to feel the wind caress your cheeks reinforced your trust when running became trustworthy. Your desire to experience floating reinforced your trust when swimming became trustworthy. You now walk, run, and swim without any doubt that life will support that experience. If you would place your attention on how life does support you, many of you would discover a new freedom to explore your passion for living. Living alongside all of your doubts and concerns are tangible reasons for trusting without knowing the outcome.

Each of you fell many times before you trusted in your ability to walk. Your desire to walk would not allow all the doubts and concerns to interfere with becoming a walker. Trust had its way with you, and you loved it! Trust is a major deposit in your energetic bank account. It reinforces all of your dreams and visions. Now you are desiring to experience your soul nature coexisting with your past history as a human being. Once again, humanity is telling you it can't be done. What a waste of time! Get your head out of the clouds human and start earning your worth.

This brings us to an interesting observation. We see so many of you truly desiring this new relationship. In fact, without it you feel that your life has no meaning. As your desire begins to generate the passion to bring this new relationship into your life, many of you hit the brakes. A part of you desires to experience your magnificent nature, and another part doesn't want to appear to be rubbing your newfound self worth in the face of your family and friends. Like you, they too inherited the belief that you must compete for love, that it must be earned. To receive love without any effort looks to you like throwing salt on their wounds. So you stop, put the brakes on your passion, and attempt to accommodate this new relationship by being passive. Until of course that passion begins to express itself as anger and resentment. Some of you turn to these very friends that you believe you are doing a favor and rant and scream that they just don't appreciate all the spiritual work you are doing for this whole planet.

In this new relationship, your soul nature very much enjoys being at the front of the line of life. It does not hesitate. It jumps right in to experience the wonders of its own nature reflected back. It accepts with your human condition that it will likely fall many times, and that is okay. It is not seeking an undistorted, absolutely pure representation of itself. It is offering itself in relationship with your human conditions. Humor, honesty, and integrity play a big role in this evolving dance. The next time you feel an impulse to explore something new, something outside your comfort zone, practice the art of trusting. Remind your mind of all the ways that trust "has" served you. Allow yourself to experience the pleasure of letting life serve your new desires. Can you trust how that desire will unfold in the same manner you trusted walking? If trust is lacking, you cannot force your soul nature to enter your life. You cannot force more money into your life. You cannot force more fulfilling relationships to come into your life. You cannot force yourself to become more creative. You can trust that ALL will be provided from a perspective that eludes your human nature.

In time as you learn to trust in the desires that originate from your soul nature, you will feel a new freedom to imagine new possibilities. We teach the art of being in receivership so that you may experience how life enjoys supporting you and gives your soul permission to be in your body. Your mind insists that it be shown the blueprint for this new relationship so it knows what to build. The new blueprint makes itself known to you as a "feeling." Learning to recognize your own soul nature is a skill very few humans have developed. Your soul has great compassion for all of its creations, including the mind. We are suggesting - mind - that you would serve your creator very well by trusting that.

It is with great pleasure that I, Michael, serve the new map makers of creation that reveal themselves on Earth as the new artists, teachers, and healers. Much of what you do with your life will not be recognized for its true value by your fellow human beings. We see its value and will continue to serve you with the deepest of respect. How does unconditional love dance with the conditioned human? How will the mind experience life when it allows your consciousness to co-exist in your day-to-day reality? It is truly a marvel for us to witness your gift to all of life and the emerging solution to our galactic dilemma!

Chapter Nine

Embrace Life

I, Michael, blend and merge my own unique presence with the energies of Yeshua and with the soul of our human friend called Bob. In this blending, we create a sacred triangle to remind you that this relationship is available to each and every one of you. As our presence descends into this magnificent, physical reality, we celebrate this opportunity to share with you how all of life is changing and evolving. It is a unique time in the history of creation. This time offers a profound resolution for so many souls that have yearned to return home. Yearned to feel embraced by the presence of unity consciousness which supports the existence of home or the kingdom.

We speak to you using words that are familiar and as well with another language that is being shared alongside these words. A language that the human being has all but forgotten. It is sacred, ancient and multi-faceted. It is spoken by your own consciousness before your mind is able to describe it for you. It communicates through your feelings a knowingness that does not doubt its nature. We invite those in this room and all that will be reading these words to also feel what is not being spoken. For these words can only inspire you to allow this presence into your life.

It is with great joy then that we enter this part of your planet that is enjoying the vibrant qualities of spring. We relish merging our presence with different aspects of Gaia, feeling the new growth, blossoming potentials and the unyielding passion to become more of what is. Within her nature, we are often drawn to the family consciousness of trees. Such a grand example of beings who never waver from being in receivership. We feel their roots descend deep into the rich body of Gaia that serves as a foundation to support their lofty perspective. It brings us much joy to feel how the family of trees fully embrace life. As their roots descend, it is not uncommon that they encounter the family of rocks. It might appear that these rocks are denying or interfering with the growth of the tree. If this were true, perhaps the trees would simply raise their limbs and declare - "Woe is me, I have encountered a hard place in my life. If these rocks aren't removed or destroyed, we trees will perish." But the tree does not feel betrayed by life simply because it has encountered a hard place in its growth. The sweet, tender roots of the tree accept the rocks. They embrace life, all of life and find a way to coexist with the rocks. The tree does not ask life to provide a map that would allow it to see the path of least resistance for its own growth. The tree embraces the mystery of life. The tree doesn't force itself upon the rock, it trusts that life will support it.

We also find great joy in merging and blending with the family consciousness of flowers. At this time of year, they open their fragile, delicate petals that expose the very heart of their existence to the intensity of light. They expose themselves to all the elements of life. We have yet to meet a flower that hesitated opening itself for fear that the sun's rays would burn its delicate features. The flower doesn't ask for a weather report to determine if the direction of the wind is ideal before expressing itself. The family of flowers openly reveals their unique beauty despite the external conditions of life.

It is also our joy to blend our presence with the family of birds. It is at this time of the year that they spend so much energy supporting their newborn. They don't worry about where they will find their nesting materials or how to feed their newborn. They embrace life with a profound knowingness that life supports life. It is through these beautiful creatures that we often speak to you dear human. Humanity still makes time to listen to the song of the bird. These songs remind each of you that joy is real and sacred.

We also love to merge and blend our presence with the family of humanity to remind you that you are never alone and that each of you represent a unique aspect in all of creation. Nothing exists quite like you. You are indeed irreplaceable! We offer ourselves in relationship with each of you to remind you that each of you carry the very seeds for new growth, unrealized potentials, and unfulfilled passions.

Yeshua has spoken about the need to declare your own truth. Nature freely shares its truth - it enjoys life! The truth that you inherited from your social, political and religious institutions denies you, for the most part, this simple truth. These inherited beliefs can feel like boulders in your life. Many of you have attempted to remove them only to discover that they grew larger in size. Some of you have declared that these hard places in your life make your life miserable and intolerable. If you can't fight the boulders, then what is the point of living.

When we entered our partners life, his truth was that he was not qualified to represent these teachings. His personality was very shy, intimidated by large groups and always had difficulty speaking in front of people. His personality suggested that surely there were others far more qualified. We persisted however and for many years reminded his personality that we didn't have any problem with all of these perceived flaws in his character. A time comes in the life of a human being when they must ask themselves, is this shyness my truth? Is feeling timid and uncertain my truth? In our last meeting, Yeshua invited each of you to give a voice to your truth, and many of you were honest enough to say that you don't know what your truth is. To discover your truth, many of you feel it is necessary to unravel your personal story, one page at a time, to expose the lies you have inherited. We ask you, is this really your truth? Do you believe that you will find your soul nature by re-living your past?

There is another way. It doesn't require any of you to do battle with the hard places in your life. We simply ask, are you willing to embrace life? Are you willing to befriend nature, and also trust that life loves to support itself?

Being in receivership invites you to recognize how you do receive from life with each breath. Are you willing to experiment by placing your attention on your inbreathe and "feel" how life does support you? Practicing this very simple but potent exercise will radically change your experience of life. You will discover that when you place your attention on being in receivership it naturally puts you in the moment. You will also discover that very few human beings choose to live in this moment. They are preoccupied by their past failures and their yet to be experienced future. You will discover an aspect of yourself that uses your past as a distraction. When you are disconnected from being in the moment, this aspect likes to pretend that it is the creator of your life.

Every time you embrace life and choose to consciously become aware of what you are inhaling into your life, you discover a great treasure that only exists in the moment - consciousness. Such a simple and harmless exercise and yet its impact is profound. Shifting your attention to "being" in receivership and using your breath as a focal point will place you directly in front of a very large boulder. This hard place in your life is called your mind!

Inhaling life with all of your heart will ask of you on a daily basis, what is my truth? Your mind holds your heart hostage when it assumes responsibility for your life. It terrorizes your ability to trust by constantly replaying memories of your past. It feeds upon a life that it perceives to be outside of itself to support its own agenda. It suffers from a self-inflicted wound until one day it is confronted with a new truth. Consciousness is indeed its creator. She has no agenda. She will not force herself into your life, but she does carry with her all of the solutions to all of the problems that torment your mind. She comes into your life each and every time you place your attention on receiving her presence. I, Michael and Yeshua do not inhale oxygen to support our life, but we do consciously inhale life that supports our truth. The mind, your male nature, is faced with a very uncomfortable truth - all is healed when the mind serves consciousness.

We spoke of this year as being a time for great change. The greatest change occurs when you stop battling the hard places in your life. Are you willing to start receiving the solutions you desire without knowing how it will change your life? Unlike your mind, consciousness is not limited by time and space. Your mind considers consciousness to be a form of magic. It is your mind that wants to describe these messages as being channeled. It uses that term to separate itself from this relationship. In time, the mind will trust its place in this new relationship. Embracing a truth that we, your non-physical counterparts, are also YOU.

Each of you now have the capacity to choose your own experience and yes, it is indeed a choice. Shifting your allegiance from your mind to your consciousness is a profound quantum leap. A choice that will ignite your inherent gift to receive whatever your heart desires. You must choose, are these thoughts that deny me joy - my truth? Is living in my past my truth? Does nature, Gaia, reflect a truth that also applies to me? Can I trust, simply by remembering to inhale life that my past can be healed? Indeed it can if you allow the feelings from your past to also be on the receiving end of what you are consciously inhaling - life! If you stop breathing, your body will certainly die. When you stop receiving, your life becomes predictable, dull and easy to control by the collective fears of humanity.

There exists the opportunity within each of you to experience love and fear, complete opposites coexisting to create a unique form of unity consciousness here on Earth. Unity consciousness, the very heart of the kingdom comes to you - breathe it in! There exists the potential to claim a freedom that cannot be extracted from your soul. It is a freedom that allows you to choose to experience the gift of being a creator. You have already tasted the co-creative abilities of your mind when it separates itself from creation. Consciousness offers itself to be in relationship with the mind as a gift.

It is a grand choice. The family of trees stands tall to remind you of your own inherent nature. They are but an extension of this magnificent soul you call Gaia who allows you to walk upon her body simply to experience a reflection of your self. Imagine the joy as you shift your attention on each inhale embracing life. Imagine experiencing being in the moment. Experiencing renewed vitality, passion and abundance. Experience the gift of now to consciously co-create your reality. Experience all of the solutions to all of the challenges that face your life. Experience your extended family, living side by side, never to feel alone again. Every breath is but another opportunity to reconnect with your own divinity, a new truth and the peace your desire. It's been a good fight, mind, but enough is enough!

Chapter Ten

Living Outside your Story

We are so honored to once again serve the physical aspect of our spiritual family. We bow before those who volunteered and have chosen to be at the forefront of change altering potentials that do not honor the sacredness of life. These times offer such a dramatic view of a reality in transition. Indeed, all of life is constantly changing and there are also cycles that encourage profound shifts. You, beloved human, are serving such a cycle with your presence here on Earth.

Your Olympics provided a stage for how this transition is changing your world. While athletes performed, a new door to freedom was opened in the land called China. She opened herself to your world community with a deep sense of pride for all that she has accomplished. The willingness to freely express a love for life opens the hearts and minds of humanity, restoring a sense of trust and wellbeing. Living alongside this fresh wind of change is also the history of this land. It is now faced with a very important question, can freedom be contained? Can such a freedom that allows full expression of the human spirit be realized within your personal and collective story?

Shortly after your Olympics, the world was treated with another emerging voice for change in the U.S. democratic convention. A dynamic speech was giving on behalf of a new, emerging culture within a country that has been granted the honor to model true freedom. As millions listened to this voice for change, humanity paused for a moment, experienced the joy of such a potential and the fear that such a life will not be chosen. Many have spoken in your past on behalf of freedom with the same clouds of fear lingering above their voices. Many of you ask, what can we do as individuals to support and empower the birthing of this inherent right for all people on Earth.

We have talked for some time of how your service to humanity included fully immersing yourself into the drama/trauma of human affairs. That experience helped to form a unique human identity that also forged a bond with your planetary family. A time would come in your life when you would awaken from that experience and would break this bond that has kept you separate from your true identity. You have called this shift a spiritual awakening, and we have come to remind you once again that the time is happening - now!

Dear reader, you did not incarnate on Earth to only experience the limitations of your past. You volunteered to demonstrate how a human being can free itself from these polarized, internal issues by walking outside the story of your life. Very few individuals have taken that walk and never before has a collective group chosen to walk this together. Many of you still wonder why we, your angelic family insist on kissing your feet. Many of us have never experienced being separate from source. We cannot imagine how painful that must be and yet here you are reclaiming that relationship with your own soul nature in service to humanity which allows them to make a choice. It is a choice that they must make for themselves.

2008 represents enormous opportunities that will energetically support your intention to experience the ex-

panded version of YOU. By itself, 2008 will simply be another year on your human calendar. The many benefits this
year has to offer resides in your willingness to challenge
your own story. Trusting in the fragile nature of a new belief that suggests life "wants" to serve you. Life is waiting at
this moment to serve your heart's desire but you must consciously choose how "you" want to be served.

Now, we often hear, how do we accomplish this?
We suggest you begin by asking yourself, how would you
like life to support you? How would YOU like to feel about
life? If you could choose how you wanted to feel, what
would you choose? Was there a time in your life when you
experienced joy? If not, can you imagine how that would
feel? See if you can bring that feeling back to you at this
moment. We are inviting you to become so vulnerable, so
open to the possibility that joy is real. Begin to breath the
energy of that feeling into your body with every breathe
you take. You might notice a change within a few minutes
or it might take all day. Continue breathing no matter what
comes up. You often say to us that if it is truly this simple,
why are there so few living their life in joy and abundance?
Indeed, excellent question! Let's shed some more light on
the choice before you.

Conscious breathing places you in the moment,
with very little effort. This simple but profound shift in

your attention to your breath will establish a new foundation of support that will also serve to work with all those feelings that have nothing to do with joy. Using your breath as a point of focus to "claim" how you want to feel will naturally change your relationship with all of life in a dramatic fashion. Your feelings represent the "being" part of you.

The work shows up when your story begins to interfere with this process, resisting the change and attempting to distract you with thoughts that live outside of joy. Fortunately, your story does not have the power to stop your breath. With a little practice, this moment will become just as real as your past. You will rediscover the joy of feeling your soul nature. Being in this moment puts you outside the story of your life. There is nothing wrong with your story, but over time you begin to realize that it doesn't know how to dance with the immense presence of your soul. It feels inadequate, clumsy and awkward.

2008 represents an opening for change. It will not be the only opening but it does offer an ideal time to reclaim your core identity. Many of you have worked so hard to experience the true nature of your soul and will naturally ask, could it really be this simple? Choose to feel alive, breath that feeling into your body, continue breathing and go live your life? Hmm! Not much drama involved in this new story and very little trauma from feeling unworthy or undeserving. In fact many would describe being in the moment as also being boring. The presence of joy has the capacity to unify life including the many aspects of your soul that reside throughout all of creation. Many of you will begin to feel that your life also serves a much bigger picture. Reuniting these aspects of your soul is your galactic service.

Now, there is nothing to feed the anxiety of your story when you choose to place your attention on your breath. We repeat, conscious breathing does not rely on your past to support itself. It will naturally blend with Christ consciousness. As we look at all the support networks that have been put into place to accommodate your story and its need to feed on life, we feel a great deal of compassion for all of you that have chosen to awaken from this dream. This will be an enormous transition that will most likely frighten your human personality, for it has no experience of a united consciousness. Self love continues to play such a vital role in this transition.

You, dear reader, volunteered to inspire your human family to walk and live outside their own story. Your human nature will proclaim that we, your non physical family, must be mistaken. Surely there are others far more qualified than yourself to represent this radical new freedom. We know who we are speaking too. The teachers on Earth at this time are all proclaiming the same words - this is your time! You already sense or feel the unsettling energies of humanity as they begin to question, collectively, their own freedom. The majority of people will most likely sit with these feelings until 2009 which invites an outward expression of these inner questions. 2012 represents an opportunity for every human being to make a choice. Freedom is your birthright, claim it within yourself to serve your external conflicts.

Some believe their freedom is being withheld by others and will choose to confront or oppose those outside of themselves. Your history is full of these conflicts. Humanity has worked very hard to achieve a sense of equality for all of its world citizens. We are inviting each of you to ignite the same passion and attention you place on events outside of yourself to your own inner process. Thoughts that continue to reinforce your old story deny YOU your freedom on a daily basis. The freedom to be a conscious, co-creator does not exist in the story of humanity's past. True freedom comes from "knowing" that you have the ability to experience life as you desire that for yourself. Life has no choice but to serve and reflect the energy of your life based on how you "feel" about your life.

2008 is a prime time to live again as you have never lived before. If you are feeling frustrated by the lack of changes in your life, make choices that challenge your story. That story can become very hypnotic by denying the value of trust and the virtue of change. Now is not the time to procrastinate. This moment, right now is why you incarnated. Celebrate it!!

Together, we promised to come back into your life to remind you of the choice that is now before you. No matter your choice, we will continue to serve you with all our love. Can you feel the warmth of your spiritual family waiting to embrace you and the joy of your own divinity waiting to ignite a new passion for living. You have endured and survived the pain of love being withheld as a human being. That qualifies you to now serve the wounded heart of your human family. You already know your story cannot serve the immense presence of your soul. It has never experienced unconditional love. The clarity and confidence you desire will build with every breath and with every intention to consciously breath joy back into your life. Kicking and screaming, your human personality will learn to trust in your soul's ability to create a fulfilling and rewarding life.

The curtains are rising to reveal part two of this grand play of consciousness on Earth. Humanity doesn't recognize this new act. It is being performed by familiar faces with a profound new joy in their hearts. Sitting in the seats alongside humanity is the presence of many spiritual families who are also waiting to see who and what is behind the curtains. How does the divine nature of a soul in a human body express itself? Everyone is holding their breath as the new actors take the stage. All of life is waiting on your next choice and I, Michael, along with many others have been invited to play alongside each of you. Suddenly, a voice behind the curtains proclaims, "I choose joy!" Fireworks explode, the curtain fully rises revealing the new players on Earth and finally, finally the new story begins! Welcome to the second coming beloveds and you thought someone else would be playing your part - silly human!

Chapter Eleven

The Christ Seed

As your planet enters the time of harvest, take a moment to commend yourself for all the potentials you planted in your life this year. Perhaps you were hoping that most of them would be ripe for picking at this time. Indeed, we admire your optimism and remind you to be patient. The seeds that you have planted within this Earth have a long-term value. Many of these potentials will be harvested by future generations. That doesn't mean you should deny yourself the reflection of your own magnificence. The dynamic nature of your soul does not seek instant gratification. It has the wisdom to embrace the long-term benefits of integrating the presence of its consciousness within the cells of your biology. We use the term dynamic to imply "continuously moving or changing; full of energy."

At this time, you can feel Gaia taking a long, deep breath. She feels your desires, your joy and begins to integrate that energy into her own consciousness. It is indeed a beautiful, co-creative process. Her presence is all around you waiting to reflect your heart's desire. Her gratitude for sharing your thoughts with her, on a daily basis, can be overwhelming if you allow yourself to truly feel her love for you. She knows that for most of you this is your last visit upon her body. As you celebrate moving your consciousness into new frontiers, she wishes to express how much she will miss "being" with each of you. She asks, "can you stop for a moment to feel my love? Dear human, you are so busy giving of yourself, come sit by me next to a tree, a stream or under the stars and allow me, Gaia, to love you back. It is a love that overflows from my own consciousness, supporting my own magnificent nature." We thank Gaia for joining us.

There was a time when many on your planet would participate in rituals to honor the changes of the seasons. Those were important times to reflect upon the cycles of creation within yourself. These rituals served the intention to feel interconnected with All That Is. We notice there is a reluctance in the collective consciousness of humanity to observe these cycles. They choose to avoid the gift that Gaia freely shares which is to "feel" your own consciousness reflected back to you to discover that life is always expanding. That level of support has increased dramatically over the last 50 years as so many of you have taken to heart that your inner reality is always the one painting your life for you. As we move into what we call Part 2 of your life, you will notice how easy it is to play and work with the energetic aspects of creation. Part 1 was all about accommodating the collective consciousness and immersing yourself into the bosom of duality and assuming a variety of roles in this polarized play on Earth. You became such accomplished actors and actresses that you even convinced yourself that you had become that role. You also convinced your fellow humans and they believe that you, like them have to work very hard to receive so little. Part 1 was a huge success in that you look very credible having endured many of the same hardships that others have experienced. Many incarnate still caught in the cycles of cause and effect. You are here to introduce the next cycle.

Part 2 is the awakening of the Christ seed within you. The Christ seed is the creative expression of All That Is. It seeds itself upon the canvas of your thoughts. Creating a tangible reflection for All That Is to perceive its own reflection. The Christ seed ensures a continuous presence of Spirit, forever growing and changing within the hearts and minds of each soul. You, soul, carry this seed and are a gift to all of life. You represent God's passion, its joy to allow its creative abilities to fully manifest. The anti-Christ is a state of mind. It is not a being. It makes its presence known by resisting the continious flow of life. Such a mind rejects its counterpart, the heart of creation and attempts to maintain an illusion of control by diminishing the presence of All That Is. The anti-Christ pushes against the natural flow of creation thereby creating a division within reality that many now call duality. The anti-Christ is not evil, it is however very insecure. You have tasted this conciousness here on Earth. It is reminding you that you are not the role you have played, and it is inviting you to become a conscious creator on this stage called Earth. This is a role that very few have witnessed on your planet. Although the Christ seed naturally works with all of life, it does not resonate with the conditions and parameters that gave birth to the role you played in Part 1.

The Christ seed has awakened within the "masters and priestesses," and it is inviting you to step forward and embrace this consciousness. It offers a radically different perspective of life. Its growth relies on trust and acceptance. You can feel its presence growing in every cell of your body. Many of you are also experiencing within your biology a community of cells that do not resonate with this energy. These cells are advocating for their own life which is supported by the role you played in Part 1. In this way, the Christ seed, change itself, is serving you very well. We know many of you feel that life isn't responding to your wishes and desires, and we very much want you to know how to create the life that YOU want for yourself. Many of you have invested most of your adult life playing these outdated roles. We see you acknowledging the presence of the Christ seed emerging in your life and attempting to accommodate that consciousness within the old role you have been playing. Sometimes you become very angry and begin to curse the heavens when you realize that the consciousness of the Christ seed is not compatible with the consciousness you have been playing so well.

Let's then take a moment to truly honor that role. May we present our own awards ceremony. You deserve the recognition for playing this role of a diminished human being. Allow us to hand you a magnificent oscar for being the best at whatever role you played. You played many leading parts that subscribed to the belief that something greater than yourself created the script. So please, indulge us as we hand out these most cherished symbols as a way to thank you for playing this game so well. Together, let's take a deep breath and review the "new" script that has just been handed to each of you. You can play any role you desire, for as long as you like in this new play. The script is based on a self empowered, fully conscious human being. It allows the presence of the soul to merge with the cells of the body which has awakened the Christ seed within. Your human family, your parents, siblings, husbands, wives and children have never seen this movie before. They have read about it, but for most of them it sounds too much like a

Walt Disney movie. For many of you, this new script begins to once again stir your passion. Becoming a self empowered human being? So few have played that role and for those that did, you believe you could play it much better. Good for you! We believe in you and sit at the edge of our seats now waiting for this new performance.

Sometimes during this new play called Part 2 of your life, you feel our presence begin to wane as if we are leaving the theater. We remind you that we came to watch the movie called the "Self Empowered Human." If we start to see trailers from old movies pretending to be this new script, like many of you, we become bored or disinterested. Our passion, like yours is in immersing our presence with the Christ seed to help it grow and become the expanded version of your own consciousness. The role that you played so well in Part 1 of your life took on an identity of its own. It feels rejected by this new script. We encourage you to allow this identity to now play the role of the photographer. It is a very honorable role, one that allows Part 1 to coexist with Part 2. Its new role is to witness and observe your new life, taking photos and arranging them in a photo album for future reference.

This is where we find so many of you at this time. You feel this immense energy as the Christ seed grows within you and you are so frustrated when you are unable to manipulate its presence into the role you played in Part 1 of your life. We invite you to become more flexible and gracious in your new role - accepting a new opportunity to now play the most incredible role of your life. This new role may or may not fit into the life you have created, it is entirely up to you. This new script does however demand all of your attention to play it out to its fullest potential. Part 2 is a fluid, open, and expanding identity that uses "change" as its foundation. Change becomes the "soundtrack" in Part 2. It is the energetic, supporting cast, which is very, very different from Part 1.You find yourself so drawn to this new role because the script is blank. You write the script as you go. There is no director or producer overseeing this new movie. You have complete freedom with unlimited resources to make your life whatever you want it to be. You just have to stop relying on the identity you created in Part 1.

Are we up for this, dear human? There is a rather large audience of nonphysical observers waiting in line to watch your new movie. Some of them are asking,"can we also play a part in this new play? This looks incredibly exciting, perhaps you will allow the presence of your nonphysical families to weave in and out of this adventurous play." In Part 1 - I, Michael, played the part of your protector. What part will you have me play in your new life? Can we be friends without swords? Interesting, sounds like a grand bumper sticker!

We leave you with these thoughts and invite you to imagine playing this new role. A role that only the finest

actors in all of creation could pull off. On a final note, may
we suggest that you stop taking all of this newness so seri-
ously. Celebrate dear human! How wise of each of you to
recognize when a movie has become boring. Now is the
time to hold that new script in your hand and begin to
imagine. What do you want your life to become? What do
you really, really, really want to experience and are you
willing to immerse yourself completely into it? We have
already bought advanced tickets, we've seen some of the
trailers and now are waiting for the grand unveiling of the
greatest show on Earth. The dynamic presence of your soul
having its way with physical reality, ah, a true love affair!

Chapter Twelve

The Room of Light and Dark

* transcribed and edited from a live channeled session

This is a grand moment for us. Each of you have invited us to go deeper with these teachings. We have been talking of how to embody your birthright - God consciousness. How to become a human being that understands that your natural state of being is a state of joy. How this planet was a place for you to find resolution with all the things that you have experienced since you left home - the kingdom so that you can bring back into your personal experience that which you feel was left behind in the kingdom.

Making that your tangible reality, your new identity, based in joy, will ask each of you to do something quite extraordinary. It will ask you to make a new pledge in your life. Tonight we invite you to give your allegiance to joy. What would happen in your life with such a commitment to joy? A commitment that would ask you to stop reacting to a reality that has nothing to do with joy. It is this sovereign stance that will ask you to affirm on a daily basis that your choice of how you would choose to feel is not negotiable.

And so it is to become conscious of your thoughts by noticing how you are feeling. Pay attention to each emotion that runs through you that is a part of your conditioning, part of the parameters that you accepted to survive being here as a human being. And yet those very parameters do not allow the magnificence of your own consciousness to be present in this moment.

You sit here tonight feeling once again exhausted from trying to accommodate what humanity is serving – less than yourself, less than your own magnificence, less than joy itself. Your body says "this doesn't feel so joyful." How can the body and your soul accommodate this new relationship - body and soul, having a mutual understanding that your allegiance to joy is now your standard for how you choose to feel. When you wake up in the morning, starting tomorrow, what will be the first tradeoff that breaks that allegiance?

What will be the first compromise that denies you the birthright to represent the magnificence of who you are. We are not judging any of you. We are asking you .... must it be this way? You already feel how painful it is to be less than who you already are. And how is this going? Have you had enough? Truly, have you had enough? How many more days must you live convincing yourself that you must try even harder to be less than what you already are - joy.

In a way you prostitute yourself by trying to accommodate the expectations you adapted to. By adapting to those expectations, you prostitute your own soul. For it knows its truth to be this joy. Even if you are the only one on the planet being truthful to yourself, at least "you" will be having a good time.

Remember that your experience on Earth is all about creating solution to all the feelings that we have experienced since we left home, since we experienced for the first time feeling separate from joy, from love. No one has done anything wrong. God/Goddess simply asked; would you go on a journey, on an adventure where love is not contained, and we all raised our hands. Like joyful children do, we stepped out into the grandness of this void, and for the first time experienced fear - feeling separate from home.

But here we are on Earth as human beings having slowed down our own thought process and call it physical reality. Slowed it down so that we could not escape our relationship to our own feelings - be they love or fear. No more running off into the 24th dimension but finding here on Earth the opportunity to finally make peace with those aspects of ourselves that feel polarized, that feel separate, diminished, unloved, and unwelcome.

Those aspects are here tonight asking: must we be responsible for holding that which is not joyful for the rest of your days? When do we get to reunite into the family consciousness that is our heritage as well? Tonight perhaps? Let's begin with loving the self and see how this feels.

Let's close our eyes together as a group and put our hands right on our hearts. (Every one takes a deep breath here.)

Begin to slowly rock back and forth, back and forth begin to just allow yourself to feel that the one that you have been searching for to love you is right here now. It is you, loving you. We invite you to fall deeply in love with yourself. Hold yourself with such affection. Hold yourself so tenderly. Hold yourself with such compassion.

Finally in all the lifetimes that you have been living as a physical human being, the search to find another to love you stops here tonight. You have found YOU. You have always been here. Let yourself feel the most profound af-fection for you – from You - for the journey that you have taken, for all the bumps and bruises.

Gently with your hand caress your face ever so lightly, like a feather touching yourself with such a tender affection. Can you say to yourself - I am beautiful? Can you say this to yourself? Can you say it to yourself - I am perfect just the way I am, and I love who I am? Can you say this to yourself and mean it from the deepest part of your heart? I am perfect just the way I am.

I am the grandest soul who has ever experienced life just as I am experiencing it here and now. I am this grand. The truth of who I am is that I am spirit also, and I have fallen deeply in love with myself.

Now open your eyes for a moment. We know you do not like this, but bear with us. So, you to you, (Michael pointing to each person to look at another) look at each other. Look at the grandness of spirit looking back at itself. Perhaps you can say to each other; if not for the love I have for myself, I would say you are the most beautiful thing I have ever seen. (Laughter here). Indeed. Keep these eyes open. Keep these eyes open and look at the one looking at you.

Can you say you are absolutely beautiful. And can you see that when you see that beauty within yourself, how this other person suddenly is more beautiful then they have ever looked before.

Indeed. Now. Allegiance to this pledge will ask of you to love yourself in such a way that it will look vain to those who have yet to learn about self love. If you are willing to love yourself in this way, you will not accept anything that would ask of you to diminish your allegiance to this joy.

The joy is what supports you. The joy is what provides the abundance, prosperity, the fulfilling intimate relationships. It is the joy that makes you irresistible to anyone. And then you can have anything you want, but you must first pledge your allegiance to this joy.

We know how much you love your Monday mornings. Tomorrow is yet another Monday. How will your day begin? It begins with an opportunity to feel so passionate about your new pledge. An allegiance to joy that is not for sale. And you will be tested. You will be tested by those that have been conditioned, like you to love themselves from a place of compromise and sacrifice.

This allegiance to your joy is so profound that it would ask of you never to sacrifice that joy for anything. You know about the personality now. You know how it is that it goes into all of its drama and trauma when it is not in the backseat. When it finds itself in the front seat of

122

your life, it goes into fear, and that is the first signal to tell you to put it in the backseat. (Laughter)

Then the joy resounds. Then the joy becomes your primary relationship. Then there isn't the need to project your needs upon others hoping that they will fulfill for you what you have not tasted for yourself - loving yourself. This unique gift from your own heart will share itself with the rest of your planet. It knows it is being supported by a continuous flow of love from the source of life.

When humanity is ready to truly question their own reality, will your foundation be so secure that you cannot be swayed. Will you allow your heart to be tampered with. This allegiance to joy is no longer secondary to all the other agendas that have created your personal story. Your personal story is your personal history. You use that personal story as an excuse for why it is that you cannot give allegiance to this joy. The personal story will tell you all the ways that joy has been denied, all the ways that humanity will not respect you if you embrace that joy.

In the past, we would engage in battle. You feared that something would be taken from you if you embodied the preciousness of your own soul - the magnificence of your own soul. You have this conditioned belief from your soul's journey that when you are in your bliss, others try to extract that energy. They do not know bliss, and you begin to feel like a commodity. Creating a new story doesn't allow others to disrespect your sovereign nature.

These grand battles are coming to an end. Even those that you are battling are weary of the battle. They are counting on all of you to create the solution here on Earth so that they too can find that joy in their own time, so that they can discover and participate in a reality that is not polarized. The new paradigm is self love. Without self love, your new story has no foundation.

When you allow love to be in your life, your body begins to radiate that presence for everyone to feel, and it is effortless. It is effortless. As soon as they want to dance to that old song that is all about pain and suffering, you respectfully say no thank you. You begin to recognize that it offers no solution to the dualistic nature of your galactic dilemma.

For you female genders – self love can be difficult. All that you inherited, all the conditioning of sacrifice, the feelings of guilt reside deep within you. As much as you intellectually feel you have liberated yourself by becoming more mindful, your heart reminds you that the embodiment of your female nature, the Goddess herself is served by your mind, your male nature.

This game, of pretending not to be your soul has finally turned the corner. We deeply honor all of you for your willingness to acknowledge this diminished human personality that refuses to trust in joy, refuses to receive the love that is available to you here and now. The solutions you seek to all of the problems that face this planet will not be discovered if you continue to sacrifice, compromise and negotiate your passion for living. Nor can you force those that do not understand how to love themselves to start to value their life. In time and by their own choice they will discover that life is sacred. You already know this, it is your time to begin to live this truth with all your heart.

Will you claim this to be your time? Will you claim that it is your birthright to embody the angelic consciousness of who you are? Can you allow your soul nature to reclaim this sacred relationship within your body?

Monday morning will arrive tomorrow. It is creeping up on you. What are you going to do with this? Does your new week begin with the same the routines or do you wake up and declare your sovereignty and your allegiance to joy?

What choices would you make if you felt free to choose anything? What would you choose? What will you choose? Some of you have already made this choice. Profound choices that would change your relationship with everything in your life.

Some of you are about to be faced with those choices, and you are beginning to feel the fear. The fear of the unknown that suggests - if you make this choice for joy how will you support yourself. The fear asks, show me a model of a self fulfilled human, and I just might consider allowing such a choice. We remind you that for most of you the only reflection you will see will be from yourself.

Beloveds, we look here at the future teachers, even though your knees are weak and they shake a little when we say this. You ask yourself, "how will we do this?" How will we serve humanity? Who among us will share our unique gift when humanity is pleading for relief from feeling the anxiety of a reality that has provided no solutions?

There will not be group celebrations and massive rock concerts to celebrate the new awakening. It will happen very quickly, and those that begin to question their own life will not have 30 years to procrastinate. Can we really be in that joy or must we change the world first before we feel we deserve to have that joy? Your service to your personal joy will support the solutions.

Every experience that you have impacts all of creation. All of creation then dances with what you resonate with within yourself. If it is not joy, then you are inviting an orgasmic pity party into your personal life. How is that going?

We have come here to remind you that you do indeed have a choice. You can embody the solution to our galactic dilemma. It is not all on your shoulders. We offer our support if you are open to receiving it. It is for you then to discover that you are representing a collective consciousness. Some of you may feel familiar with the Family of Michael or Sananda. Some of you prefer other families. It matters not. But you do not need to do this alone, nor was it intended that you do it alone.

The one that feels that it is doing it alone needs to get in the backseat so that you can experience the collective love descending into the cells of your body. What will the choice be when you awaken tomorrow? What will you do differently with your life that gives credibility to this allegiance to joy? How will you accommodate it?

We will be watching. Not with any judgment but for the opportunity to ask; are you ready to truly enjoy your life. There is no need to wait any longer. As soon as you make that choice for joy, we will celebrate and together you will feel the love that binds us. We are not the voices that condemn, judge, or belittle. We are the quiet thoughts within you that ride on waves of passion. We are the ones that whisper; can we play now.

There have been a few who have embodied this solution. There have been a few who have tasted it, and humanity – hmmm, well you know the story. You have come here in the millions. There are 3 percent of you now on planet Earth, and we know your mind says well when it is 50 percent maybe we will risk the chance.

It is a priceless thing you are trading. This joy is so priceless. It is a jewel that cannot be controlled. Nobody would trade it in if they allowed themselves to taste it. Nobody would ever consider tarnishing this jewel. Once you allow yourself to love yourself this profoundly, you cannot imagine anyone more perfect than you being with you.

So, it is time to take you on a journey. We are going to go very deep tonight. It is not intended to shake anybody up. It is intended to wake you up. It is intended to get you out of the dream you are dreaming. There is another dream to dream, and it is solely based in joy, and those who are dreaming it also taste it, perceive it, experience it, and know that it is not tradeable for anything. This joy is not about escaping the reality you face. To the contrary, it is about facing that reality with the very solution it yearns to know. What courage all of you have simply for being here at this time!

We invite the Family of Sananda to be here with us tonight. We invite you to imagine that your life is contained within a home. This home embodies all the experiences your soul has collected since you left the kingdom. What you would call your living room, is the place where you have chosen to express yourself, where you experience life. You had the wisdom to design this living room in the shape of a circle, allowing for change in your life, the freedom to flow. Your personal identity in this living room is also greatly influenced by the adjacent rooms that face each other on opposite ends of your circular living room.

One of these rooms you call the room of light. This is where we meet many of you. You joyfully invite us to enter this room of light. It is beautiful. We enjoy your presence and your company very much in this room. We see it has four walls, and on the ceiling there is an energy that speaks of your freedom. As we walk into this room of light with you, it is here that you trust us. It is here that you are most comfortable letting us be with you. You have placed all the qualities of your soul nature, your memories of the Kingdom in this room. We are most honored that you also invite us. Like you, we too resonate with these qualities.

We see that your four walls also represent different aspects of what you call the light. We also see that these aspects change on a daily basis. One of these is called Compassion. It is a Compassion that you share with yourself for having the courage to be on Earth at this time. It is a Compassion that understands that suffering and pain is but a byproduct of feeling disconnected from your own joy. This Compassion allows others to experience life free from your own expectations. Compassion - such a powerful energy in this room, this room of light.

We see another wall that you ask us to admire. This wall you have called Self Acceptance. Here you love your own reflection as being perfect. You don't feel the need to acheive perfection. Here you allow yourself to be loved just are you are.

You turn to another wall, and share with us the energy known as Self Fulfillment. Here you make choices that truly serve your heart's desires. You don't compromise your joy or sacrifice your true value. Self fulfillment is all about being true to your love for yourself.

We turn now to the next wall, and you gladly introduce us to the energy you call Patience. This energy is all about allowing life to unfold without intervening. Patience asks of you to stop pushing against life, trusting that change will indeed happen under the guidance of your own soul.

We have visited many of you in this room of the light. This is where we play with you much of the time. This is where we come in through our partner (Bob). It is here, in this room of the light that you feel safe being in the presence of your magnificence. For the light is the perfect reflection of all the qualities you remember the kingdom to be. It is how you have learned to define reality. It represents the truth, what is good, positive, and love based. Your memory serves you well beloved, for these are some of the very qualities that supported all of life in the reality we call the kingdom or home.

Together we come back into your living room. You understand that your living room becomes a reflection of the qualities from these outer rooms. The room of the light and of course the room of the dark. You tell us you spend a lot of time in the room of light, but you don't always feel that presence in the living room or your life. You don't always feel patient, fulfilled or accepting of yourself.

We nod and ask, what is in this other room? You simply say you do not want to go in there. Is this room not connected to your life? And you proclaim again that you do not want to go in there. It is the room of the dark. Indeed, let us see together what resides in this room. You seem a little troubled that we would want to visit this room. Let's see the whole picture so that we can serve you better.

You agree to come into this room of the dark. It is your room filled with your feelings about your story. As we enter, the energy feels a bit gloomy. We notice your heart begins to feel a pain. I, Michael, offer my sword to radiate more light to discover together what is hiding in here?

It has four walls just like the room of light. As we turn to one of the walls, you stand behind us, and I read it for you. The wall says Anger. What is this Anger? Is this the same Anger we feel in your living room? Are you angry for not being able to return to the kingdom? Are you angry at God/Goddess for sharing the gift of creation with You - the gift that allows you to create your own experience in any

131

way you would desire to experience life? We invite you to honor this anger by looking into the oppostite room, the room of light. What qualities in this room would serve your anger? How would your compassion dance with your anger? We invite you to play with these oppostite qualities and discover for yourself the healing effects.

As you do this we notice the wall of anger in the room of the dark begins to turn grey. We turn to the next wall that says Self Betrayal. Indeed, there is great pain when you deny love for all aspects of yourself. Self betrayal would ask of you to blend a presence from the room of light to resolve this feeling. We see you inviting Self Acceptance and much to your surprise you begin to experience the healing effects. As you do, the room turns from dark to grey.

We notice a newfound confidence in you as we turn to the next wall. Again, we feel your pain in your heart as it reads Self Doubt. As a creator of your own experience, you have judged your choices and abilites and now feel unqualified to represent this gift of life. You feel you need more time to prefect your manifesting skills. Once again we invite you to share an aspect of yourself from the room of the Light with this feeling. You invite patience and immediately begin to experience a renewed sense of hope. You look directly into my eyes and reflect back a deeper understanding of yourself. It is beautiful!

And now you seem quite excited to show us the fourth wall. Resentment. You seem to enjoy being able to share your story. Yes, resentment, you resent having the freedom to become a soveriegn, independant soul if it brings you so much pain. Life in the kingdom was always united with all the qualities in your room of light. You never once experienced pain, doubt or anger. You have discovered something profound. The qualities of Light or the Kingdom will come to you no matter what enviroment you find yourself in. You again invite another aspect of your light and share it with this resentment and witness these complete oppostites are served by your Light. Once again the wall becomes grey.

On the ceiling of this room I point my sword and ask you to read what it says. Feeling a little confused, you read the word Freedom. Hmmm. You take our hand and led us back into your living room. Together we see the tangible reflection of your relationship with the room of the light and dark. You have fallen in love with life having discovered the solution to your galactic dilemma.

Now you understand, you see the relationship within yourself with eyes unclouded. You see by your unwillingness to acknowledge the existence of the dark, you have created a dualistic experience within yourself. None of those feelings existed in the kingdom and yet your perception of life outside the kingdom indeed now includes fear.

133

You see by using the very qualities of life that bring you joy and sharing them with those aspects that are in a lack of joy, you heal the separation.

A new journey then begins for each of you. It is the Masters who understand that your soul nature has changed since you left home. The qualities of God/Goddess while in the kingdom only embodied the light. They do not know fear for they never experience life as being separate. They do not know the room of the dark, but they accept it is real for you. They know of your reaction to leaving Home. Facing the void itself brought up many new feelings for all of creation. They continue to love you but now remind you that love doesn't come "from" them, it is within you supported by their presence.

So, it is to be this clear now. Can it also be your joy to become conscious of all your feelings and begin to take responsibility for how it is that you want to feel? This will challenge your allegiance to joy. Acknowledging your polarized, internal relationship will expand your experience that then allows for ecstatic, joyful states of consciousness to become your reality.

Mmmmm, are we ready yet? Can we wait? The clock is ticking. What else is there to do? It is simply to enjoy your life. Stop what you are doing in any way that diminishes your exquisite, blissful, ecstatic relationship with physical reality and turn it into a joyful relationship.

You will look vain. Too bad. It's not your problem. You are the one with the smile on your face. It is not your problem.

Let those that insist on playing in duality go. They will come to you when they are ready. They will come to you when they are pleading "how do we get out of this pain, how do we get out of this misery," and you will share – give your allegiance to joy. It does not require struggle. It doesn't need to be difficult. You already are making it difficult. Denying you joy equals difficulties. Your joy will not conform to anything that is not based on honoring the joy itself.

A lot has been stirred up here tonight. We will warn you, there will be a little detoxing here, and we know for many of you - you are sick and tired of this. Drink lots of water. A gallon a day. Bring in the gallon to your unjoyful occupations and joyfully detox yourself. Or stay at home and drink all the water you want and be in bliss. Could it be this simple? What would you have to trust?

We know all of you here tonight and many reading these words would enjoy having more abundance, money. So if you want more of this abundance to come into your life, then it is to have a healthy relationship with how money does come to you. Money comes to you when you relate to money as being a reflection of your joy. Stop labeling it with all the conditions and beliefs you have about it. Give it up. It is just a form of exchange but in duality- there are some who get it, and the rest of you have to fight over the scraps. And that feels like what?

For God/Goddess, All That Is, it is joy. And when you want that to be in your life, they ask "may we be in your life?" There was one commandment given to Moses that he forgot to write down. (laughter) Go play my children! But when you are in duality, you do not hear that voice, you hear a condemning, authoritarian father. It is now time to hear the new voice that has nothing to do with judgment or blame.

It all will change. Self love invites you to open the door to the dark rooms, to be a frequent visitor because you will learn that it is also your joy to share love with fear. For the love that you are cannot be contained in the room of the light. It cannot be contained in any room, and if you try to contain it, your body will tell you, this is hurting containing this joy. It must flow, expand and be expressed. As you trust in your willingness to express your life with all aspects of your life, your life will begin to feel more complete. We serve the completeness within each of you with joy and passion.

Chapter Thirteen

The Gift of Creation

At this moment, all of humanity is beginning to experience a very intense transition. Your human family is feeling very frustrated from relying on a conditioned identity that feels disconnected from life, disconnected from a joy and passion for living. This dramatic shift is impacting every aspect of your personal and global affairs. This shift invites each of you to reclaim your creative abilities by embracing the heart of your own soul. Your soul is calling you to jump into the river of your own passions, awakening your heartfelt desires to flow with the ongoing current of creation.

A natural part of this transition reunites your physical experience with the presence of your spiritual families. We, the Family of Michael, are but one of many families or expressions of source energy. Each of you have a very intimate relationship with these galactic families. Your experience on Earth also serves as a spiritual reunion for all families of consciousness.

Supporting this reunion is a profound sense of love. It is a love that accepts life as being perfect just as it is in this moment. It is not waiting for you to resolve your inner conflicts. It is not concerned about your unfulfilled desires. It truly accepts you as being perfect for all that you are right now.

We hear many of you say, why does it take us so long to trust in such a love. We would say when your conditioned nature stops fighting with your soul and allows the beauty of this moment to exist, then much will be revealed to each of you. For in this moment exists the love we are describing. In this moment exists YOU, your soul! We know it can be very frustrating living inside this conditioned self that feels disconnected from the soul. Be patient with yourself. Remember to breathe in the presence of your soul nature. The moment brings you a clarity that you can trust. It allows you to confidently make choices without the need to second guess your intentions. There is a love waiting for you beyond anything you have tasted as a human being. It is profound!

Stop Fighting with your Soul

When you stop fighting with the presence of your soul, that choice becomes a life altering decision. Many of you have come to realize you don't need to die to experience this type of love. You can have your cake and eat it right here on Earth. It is a choice that allows an unconditional love to be in your day-to-day reality. It allows you to actively use the gift of creation and begin to accept yourself as being a creator each and every time you embrace this love as also being YOU. It is a choice, one that you must make for yourself.

As we blend our presence with our human counterparts, I, Michael, and my beloved friend Yeshua bow before you, the brave new pioneers of consciousness. You are the ones that have grown tired of playing the game that would deny you love. Indeed, this game has been going on for some time. This game requires that you accept a part of an oppressor or victim. No matter what role you played in all of your lifetimes here on Earth, like all games, it has an ending. Some endings call for an end to life as you know it. Indeed, each of you incarnated into this world knowing that such a possibility was very real. You knew that the game humanity is currently playing would end between the year 2000 - 2012. You accepted that Earth would most likely enter into a grand battle between forces that have invested great resources into the outcome of this game.

Such a battle would have initiated dramatic changes on your planet. Yet you still choose to incarnate and serve a love that doesn't play games.

Direct Connection with Spirit

As we look across your beautiful planet, so many are now becoming conscious vessels for the source of life. They are beginning to live and share a profound wisdom that speaks for the heart of creation. Many of you attend workshops and spiritual events to feel the presence of this energy, to hear a truth that resonates with your own heart. In your past, humanity relied on others to act as facilitators for source energy. These messengers for consciousness served your human family with a compassion that was aligned with the energetic presence of Spirit. All of your religions embrace the lives of these individuals as they were eventually translated by other human beings.

Your current messengers have access to a technology that allows the message from consciousness to be recorded, read or listened to just as it was spoken. With your internet, you can see firsthand both the conditioned nature of these channels and their unique connection to their own soul families. It is a profound shift from second-hand knowledge to witnessing for yourself a direct experience.

This profound transition is asking humanity to fulfill its hearts desires by embracing a direct relationship with the source of life unfiltered by your various institutions. Throughout your history many have found it convenient to inject the word God into their agendas without ever embodying such a consciousness. God consciousness makes no claim on life, whether that be another person, country, or a planet. It honors all of life as being sacred.

As this transition continues to unfold, many will need to ask themselves - whom do I serve? What in my life is non negotiable? What value do I place on life? Will I compromise these values? The game humanity has been playing denies the existence of an unconditional love. It relies on the mind to define its reality. It believes in a higher power while denying the physical integration of that presence.

Once again, we bow before the new leaders of consciousness. You are the ones that have chosen to use this lifetime to enhance your relationship with your soul nature and to empower your choices with a love that knows no boundaries. This has had a profound impact on all of humanity. It has shifted their attention from the habitual thoughts and released a tremendous amount of energy that was being used to support the old game - a game that many will continue to play but without the satisfaction that was anticipated. It is a choice that every human being must make for themselves.

The Law of Attraction

Your attention is beginning to shift to developing your own creative abilities. The law of attraction has made a profound impact on many of your lives. We remind you, it is not called the law of magic. It takes more than repeating words or waving wands to consciously create in physical reality. The law of attraction relies on honesty. Our relationship with many of you now allows us to be more direct. You are not asking us to do for you what you are unwilling to do for yourself. We are deeply honored each and every time you invite our presence to be a part of your life and joyfully serve the emerging creator. It's been a long time since a human being has taken responsibility for their own creative process.

We have spoken of the unique relationship that resides within every human being. The mind, body, spirit, and soul are coexisting in this shared time and space. We have explored the nature of your personality/ego and invited you to stop asking it to represent your magnificence. Of late, we described your personality as also being multi-faceted and introduced these as being some of your human aspects. These are the parts of your past that still reside within you, some that are very wounded, angry, and re-sentful.

We would like to explore these aspects from an-other perspective. For many of you have discovered that as your heart opens, you begin to feel and sometimes hear aspects of yourself that once resided in your subconscious.

Managing your Hotel

We invite you to imagine yourself living and work-ing in a beautiful and grand hotel. Your soul sits at the front desk as the manager of this magnificent hotel. Every-thing and everyone that enters passes by you.

Now, in our last discussion, we invited each of you to declare that you love your life! We invited you to dis-cover how it feels when you do declare - I love my life! This declaration has served many of you. It has ignited your imagination and inspired some of you to exercise your creative abilities.

We invited you to share these abilities and to open yourself to receiving all the appreciation that comes back to you when you do share your creations. We used the exam-ple of a product or service, but your creations are not limited to a tangible object. Any experience that left a strong, emotional impression on your life also represents a creation or an aspect of yourself. In this way, these aspects have their own identity that are based on your experience.

As a soul, you were gifted by the mother/father aspects of creation with the ability to also create life. As a human being, many of your creations become tangible or take form in the many roles you play. You are conscious of the infant, child, teenager, your gender, sexual preference, parent, grandparent, employee and employer. You experience yourself within these roles and over time the role can begin to define you. We call all of these your "guests," and all of them are currently living inside your hotel. The ones you are most conscious of and demand the most attention tend to reside on the first floor. The conscious activity of your life occurs when any of your guests visit the hotel lobby. It is here that they engage your attention, interact, blend, and merge their presence with you co-creating your day-to-day reality.

Each of your guests have their own unique identity. You can identify many of them through your habitual patterns of behavior. The image of a hotel allows us to work with your mind, but truly it is another word for your body. We have discovered in being with you that the moment we say "body," many of you emotionally disconnect from your body.

We have this magnificent soul working behind the front desk as the manager of your hotel. The name of your hotel is the same name you have on your drivers license. The collective presence of all these guests contribute to your experience of life. Humanity asks on a daily basis - who am I? At the core of your soul is a presence that knows it is living within its own creation and supports that knowing with compassion and love.

Some of your guests demand your attention on a daily basis, complaining about their life in your hotel. Everyone knows you are the manager. You spend a great deal of your time each day listening and responding to these complaints.

Some of these guests invest a lot of energy trying to convince you, the manager, that they are more qualified to run your hotel. They often challenge your wisdom or ridicule your ideas in an attempt to undermine your authority. From our perspective, the majority of humanity deals with this internal soap opera on a daily basis. Some souls simply resign their position, declaring they didn't come here to run a childcare center. In which case, the guests begin to oversee the daily operation of the hotel. The collective consciousness of all of humanity is a reflection of how each of you manage your own hotel.

Setting your Creations Free

As we watch this play unfold something dramatic is beginning to take place. Some of the managers have stopped feeling responsible for how their guests are feeling. They have chosen not to take it personally when their guests complain. They are beginning to invite some of the other guests that reside in the upper floors to join them in the lobby for a cup of coffee or a glass of wine. Some of these managers have learned to listen and respond to the daily complaints by saying – "I respect how you feel. You are welcome to stay as long as you like, but if this hotel doesn't meet your needs, you of course are free to go any-time!"

This shift is creating a quantum leap in the life of your hotel. Managers all over the world are beginning to release their own expectations, their own self judgments. They are beginning to feel a renewed sense of joy for their work. In essence, they are learning to set their creations free with the same consciousness that set them free. They are seeing how their guests are a blessing to life. They are beginning to honor the gift of creation that was freely given to them. Each of you souls are a reflection of the mother/father aspects of creation. The managers are be-ginning to truly love their guests. They are embodying unconditional love and compassion and for the first time your guests are speechless.

Your guests are all free to change, grow, and evolve within the identity you gave them through your own expe-rience of life. You deny them and yourself the natural state of expansion and growth by judging yourself and them for being less than perfect. This perfection you seek is an illusion.

Most of your guests living in your hotel are also the byproduct of a consciousness you left behind when you stopped playing that old game. The choice you made to not play in this game has most of your guests feeling abandoned or rejected. You are experiencing this same dilemma in your relationship with those that live outside your hotel. We want you to be very clear about your choice. You are not leaving anybody behind. You are simply creating your own game. Many in your hotel have heard the news. The manager has reclaimed God consciousness. Many of the guests are talking to each other - what does this mean? Will we be evicted? How does God consciousness truly relate to life?

Life in your hotel is changing. You now spend your day listening to the thoughts of the guests that live in the upper floors. They don't complain about life nor do they demand your attention. For some of you, you just gave them a key to their own room. You seem to enjoy their company, their presence and so it comes as no surprise that some of these guests are also writing these words. We, the Family of Michael, live in our partners hotel and love to play in the lobby with him on a daily basis. We haven't taken over the hotel, we gladly invite any of the other guests to sit by the fireplace, share a cup of earl grey tea while we listen to their story. It is a story that is dramatically changing because the manager has fallen in love with life.

Thank you dear human for opening your hotel to our presence, we have missed you more than you know!

Other Books by Robert Theiss

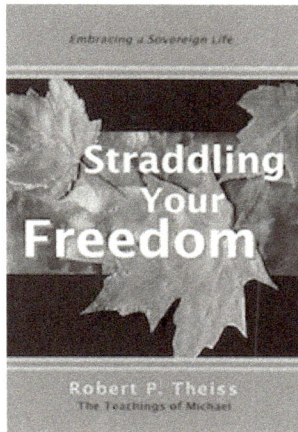

Embracing a Sovereign Life

Straddling Your Freedom

Robert P. Theiss
The Teachings of Michael

Straddling your Freedom

In his first book, Robert Theiss openly shares a spiritual journey which led him to develop a conscious relationship with Spirit and the Family of Michael. Reuniting his conditioned human nature with the dynamic presence of his soul. Straddling your Freedom explores the power of joy, the value of being in receivership and a new love for self that reunites our soul with all of life.

Paperback/ ISBN 978-0-578-00664-2 (2007)
ISBN 978-0-578-06433-8 (2010)
195 pages

Published by Ancient Wings®

www.ingramcontent.com/pod-product-compliance
Lightning Source LLC
LaVergne TN
LVHW011236080426
835509LV00005B/531